Let the Hurricane Roar

ROSE WILDER LANE

Let the Hurricane Roar

A Harper Trophy Book

Harper & Row, Publishers

Wild Plum Creek

I

WHILE they were children playing together, they said they would be married as soon as they were old enough, and when they were old enough they married. David liked to remind her that he had never asked her to marry him; he liked to see her smile sedately, as she always smiled at his teasing.

She was a quiet person. When she was a little girl she was often asked if the cat had got her tongue. Even with David she had a way of saying nothing in words. Her eyes, which could not lie, told what she felt. Before she smiled, a shadowy dimple quivered in one cheek. Her face was quiet under smooth wings of hair, and all her movements were gentle and deft. In her heart she never quite lost the wonder that she, quiet and shy and not very pretty, had won such a man as David. He was laughing and bold, a daring hunter, a dancer, fiddler and fighter.

She thought of him always as he was on summer Sunday afternoons when his family was spending the day with hers. Perhaps some other neighbors were there too.

The old men sat on the bench against the shady side of the log house, talking slowly, with chuckles and long pauses. Their sons went out to look at the calf and pigs. Children ran about, climbing the rail fence, raiding the wild-blackberry thickets. The babies slept on a faded quilt in the shade of the oak, and near them the women rested on benches brought from the house. David's grandmother swayed in the hickory rocker that bumped over the uneven ground. Everything in the clearing was drowsy till David sat down on a stump and tuned his fiddle.

His favorite hymn always lifted him to his feet. His chin left the fiddle, he shook back his thick brown hair. His voice rang out above all the other voices; it led the defiant, triumphant song that surged across the stumpy fields and echoed into the vast, unconquered forest:

Let the hurricane roar!
*   It will the sooner be o'er!*
We'll weather the blast, and land at last,
*   On Canaan's happy shore!*

Many settlers had come to the settlement in the Big Woods while David and Molly were growing up. When they married there was little good land left. Farther west, the country was not yet settled and the land was said to be rich and level, and without forests. So they went west.

David's father was an open-handed man and he had six sons younger than David; he could afford to be generous. David was not yet nineteen. His labor belonged to his father until he was twenty-one. But his father gave him his time—a free gift of more than two years. To cap this, for good measure heaped up and running over, he gave David the team and wagon he would have earned by working till he was twenty-one.

Molly's parents gave her two blankets, two wild-goose-feather pillows, and cooking pot and pan and skillet. They gave her a ham, a cheese, two molds of maple sugar, and Tennyson's Poems beautifully bound in green and gilt, with steel engravings. She had the patchwork quilts she had pieced. David had his fiddle and his gun. Their families together sent East for their Bible, and the circuit rider wrote their marriage certificate on the page provided for it. The pages for Births and Deaths were still blank, waiting to be written upon. So, well provided for, they set out to the West.

At first Molly was sad because she was leaving her family forever. She ached for the busy life with her mother and sisters in the log cabin, for her father's coming home from work or hunting, even for the oak tree by the door and the path to the spring. But these memories soon ceased to hurt her, in her happiness with David.

They could never decide which was best—the fresh mornings, when the first rays of the sun found Molly packing the washed dishes and David whistling while he hitched up the team; or the varied days of traveling westward on unknown roads; or the evenings by the camp fires.

David played his fiddle while the horses grazed and stars or moon shone overhead and the night air was sweet. Or they sat cozily together with the firelight on their faces, and talked about the things they had seen that day and the home they would have in the West. Then Molly banked the fire while David tied the horses safe for the night, and they went to bed in the wagon.

Every day David shot game. When they needed flour and tea and sugar, they camped at some settlement while he worked for supplies. Whenever he had money, he brought her a present; once a little box covered with tiny shells, a mirror set in the lid; and once fifteen yards of calico for a dress she didn't really need. She scolded him, for she was thrifty, but she never cured him of bringing her presents. He liked to see the shining in her eyes.

Late that summer they reached the western prairie and David got a job, teaming on the railroad. They were going to have a baby, and he wanted to earn money. The homestead could wait, he said; he would look around for one, and meantime she must stay in the railroad camp.

The long railroad embankment was being pushed westward. Scores of men and teams were working on it, raising a low smoke of dust under the enormous sky. The camp was small on the immense plain, where there was nothing but miles of wild grass blowing in the wind.

The bunk house, the cookhouse and the company store were all of raw new lumber. The contractor's wife had a little frame shanty, and so did her sister who ran the cookhouse, but they were crowded and Molly did not want to stay in them.

David built her a sod shanty. He cut the strips of tough sod and she helped him to lay up the walls and stretch the canvas wagon top over them. A thatch of slough grass kept out the heat of the sun. In two days the house was done, neat and cool and all her own.

David was hauling supplies to the new camp, twenty miles west. Every second night he was away from her, and she was lonely. She could not like Mrs. Baker or her sister. They were coarse, blowzy women, much older than she. She talked more to their children, who ran about bare-legged and brown, whooping and racing their bare-backed ponies over the prairie.

On nights when David was away, she lay awake a long time. A distant wolf howled. A coyote prowled softly around the shanty. The company store was noisy with boots and the rough voices of men drinking and gambling. A lonely voice went by, singing:

I've been working on the railroad,
   All the livelong day;
I've been working on the railroad,
   To pass the time away.

David had given her a gun and she was never afraid. But she wanted David to be there. The loneliness was hard to endure.

Her hands and face were brown as an Indian's from the prairie wind and sun. When she unpinned the collar of her basque, it was odd to see the brown face on the milk-white neck. David teased her: "Come here, squaw! Give me a kiss. Oh, little squaw, little squaw, your baby's going to be a papoose!"

She thought about this, sitting on his knee. "Well," she said soberly, "it's your baby too."

She never understood his shout of amusement when she said something plainly true, like that. But she knew his laughter was part of his loving her.

In September the winds were edged with cold and all day long the gray sky resounded to the signal calls of wild birds flying south. The men worked sullenly in cold winds and dust. All their wages had gone back to the company store and now the camps were closing; there would be no more work till next year. In the camp farther west there were riots about wages; men were killed. But Molly knew that David could take care of himself. He had earned money enough for the winter's supplies and for tools and seed, and he had found a homestead. His blue eyes sparkled when he told her. On this homestead there was already a dugout and barn, and fifty acres of the sod were broken. Another man had taken the land and done all that work, yet he was giving up, he was going back east. He said he could not stand another winter of loneliness.

David asked, "Would it be too lonesome for you, Molly? There wouldn't be another human being within thirty, forty miles."

"You wouldn't have to go away?"

"No, I'd be there, but——"

He did not finish the sentence, so she said, "No, I won't be lonesome."

In the middle of the night David started to the Land Office, to get that homestead before anyone else. He was not yet twenty, but he was a married man, the head of a family, so he need not wait till he was twenty-one before he filed a claim to a homestead. Molly listened to the jolting of his wagon, going away in the dark. It was thirty miles to the Land Office.

Three days went by. The sun had set; the sky was a pale, cold yellow, flushed with pink all around the rim of the horizon, when Molly heard the rattle of the wagon, far away. David was jubilantly singing. She could hear only the tune, but she knew the words:

Come to this country
*   and don't you feel alarm,*
For Uncle Sam is rich enough
*   to give us all a farm!*

She knew he had the papers. In five years they would own their land.

Work stopped in the camps. Under the lines of wild birds flying south, a stream of men was going east. In wagons, on horseback, on foot, they were going back to the settled country. The bunk house was empty and the cookhouse closed. In the chill wind Molly helped David pack supplies and take the canvas wagon top from the sod shanty. They slept in the wagon that night, and next morning David hitched up the horses and they started west. The camp was dark. Only the Bakers were busy with lanterns, loading the last of the company goods into their wagons headed east. David stopped in front of the store to say good-by.

Mrs. Baker was angry when she heard that David and Molly were not going out for the winter. She was a big, hearty woman, who cut her hair like a man's and did not wear corsets. She faced David, hands on hips.

"That child, in her condition!" she said. "You want to kill her?"

Her blunt talk frightened David. He had not supposed it was so dangerous for a woman to have a baby, but now he was ready to abandon everything and take Molly east. He agreed that she must have neighbor women with her. But Molly thought of the homestead. She knew that claim jumpers would get it; they might kill David when he came back to it in the spring.

She sat quiet until everything had been said. Then she looked at the blowzy woman. She let her eyes show that she did not think Mrs. Baker was quite a lady.

In her soft voice she said politely, "Good-by, Mrs. Baker. We must be going now."

David drove on, but he was still ready to turn back. He was perturbed. Molly was not at all troubled. "It's natural to have babies," she reminded him. "I can have ours on the homestead as well as anywhere."

When he persisted she said with finality, "I do not want anyone else there when the baby is born."

She did not speak about claim jumpers. David was so brave. he would have taken his chances with them.

Then sunshine came across the prairie and they were both light-hearted. They drove all day and met no one. Once they saw a rider in the distance, but he soon disappeared. He was perhaps an Indian, or perhaps one of the white outlaws whose hiding places were farther west. In winter weather they would not bother anyone.

All day the horizon maintained its unvarying circle around the trotting horses. The wild grass rippled in the wind. Twice David pointed out a buffalo wallow, and once they saw a loping wolf. In the afternoon they passed Lone Tree, a solitary cottonwood, a landmark for all that country, and David drove out of his way to get some seeds from it.

Just before sunset they drove around the end of a slough. A little farther on there was a sod barn. David drove by it, and suddenly the level-looking prairie split apart; the horses stopped at the edge of a chasm.

"Here we are!" David said.

Molly's eyes were round. He helped her down from the wagon, and together they stood looking down at water in the creek bed below. Looking at Molly, David laughed aloud in joy. He had kept this creek a secret, to surprise her. She hadn't known there was water on the homestead. They would not have to dig a well.

"I thought we'd name it Wild Plum Creek," David

said. Two little wild plum trees, bare of leaves and distorted by winds, stood by the water. How they had come there was a mystery. "They're alive," he said. "They'll blossom in the spring."

He could hardly wait to show her the dugout. It was under their feet. The prairie sod was smooth over it and the blown grass hid the top of the stovepipe. A path went slanting down against the steep creek bank to the doorway.

The ledge of earth before the door was narrow and could easily be kept clear of snow. The door opened into a room large enough to hold all their supplies. It was clean and neat. The floor was pounded smooth and hard, canvas covered the ceiling and part of the walls. There was a bunk, a table, a bench and an iron cookstove. David had bought them from the man who abandoned the place. Sunshine came through the doorway, which looked across the low western bank of the creek to the endless prairie and the sky. There was even a small window hole covered with oiled paper; it would let in daylight during the winters.

"Like it?" David asked unnecessarily.

"Yes," she said.

He smiled deep into her eyes and almost crushed her in his joyous hug.

Nothing could have been more cozy for wintertime, cooler in the summers. And all this coziness and comfort, the good sod barn, the quarter section of rich, treeless land, the creek, the plum trees, even a bit of slough, which would provide hay for the horses and hay to burn in the stove—all this was theirs! They need only live here and work the land, and in five years they would have the title.

Molly said, "We'll cut up our wagon top, too, and cover the rest of the wall."

Everything was snug before the blizzards came. The horses were warm in the barn, with slough hay and oats to feed them till spring. In his eagerness David had cut all the dried slough grass and the stacks stood high beside the barn.

The dugout was cozy while winds howled and the deep snow moved in drifts over the land. On clear days David went out with his gun and came back with meat and furs. Molly scrubbed and baked and washed and ironed and cooked. On days when the blizzards came shrieking from the northwest, David groped his way only to the barn and back. He had stretched a rope from the top of the path to the barn door, so he would not lose his way in the blinding storms, but Molly was uneasy until he came back safe.

Yet those days were best of all. David cleaned his gun, oiled his boots, twisted slough hay for the fire. From two packing boxes he made a cradle. He scraped the wood carefully with a bit of broken lamp chimney, till it was as smooth as his hand, and on the headboard he carved two birds and a nest. The place was gay with his whistling while he worked. Molly saved her mending and sewing for these stormy days. She worked quietly, smiling to herself. The lamplight was cheerful, the stove gave out its heat and the good smell of cooking. Then David took his fiddle from its box; he played and sang, keeping time with a patting foot. Those were festive days.

On Sundays they did not work, and David played only hymns. It was splendid to see and hear him, roaring out his favorite to the wind that howled in the stovepipe. Then Molly read to him. David was a slow reader, but he liked to listen while Molly read aloud. She read the Bible, and she read Tennyson's Poems. That winter she read the green-and-gilt book from cover to cover. It made their life even more rich and beautiful.

February was clear; the cold was so intense that the air seemed glittering ice, and the silent world was buried in snow. Molly was heavy now, and clumsy, and her breath was short. Though the weather was good for hunting, David went only to the barn and back; he would not leave her long alone. Sometimes, even when he was there, Molly heard the silence and was afraid.

The silence of those miles of snow untouched by any trace of human beings, marked only by the inhuman winds and the paws of wild animals, was without enmity or pity. Its indifference was more cruel than hate.

She tried to remember all she had heard about childbirth; it was very little. She did not let David guess how much she wanted her mother.

The pain began early one afternoon. She had set a batch of bread; she moved the pan nearer the stove so that the dough would rise more quickly. David must have food while she was unable to cook. He was

twisting hay for fuel, whistling while he twisted, dou-
bled, knotted the long strands into firm sticks, and
she was able to knead the bread and mold it into
loaves before he saw her face.

She had known the pain would be bad and was re-
solved to make no outcry. She would not make it harder for David. Indian women bore their babies silently.

That night was very long. She lay in the bunk and
smiled at David whenever she could. Even worse
than the pain was the terror. Her courage seemed so
small against the implacable indifference that possessed her body. Desperately she clung to David, but
even David was helpless. She did not scream. In the
moments when she was herself again, she was glad
and a little proud that she had not screamed. David
wiped the sweat from her face. She smiled at him and
spoke happily about the baby.

Several times she asked in surprise, "Isn't it morning yet?"

Then everything became confused. Daylight and
darkness were mixed. She heard shrieks and knew
they were hers; she could not stop them. Even David
was gone. There was nothing anywhere but unbearable agony. She herself was ebbing, going—a last little
atom fighting, failing——

The baby was born in the morning of the second
day.

For a long time she knew that she was lying under
eyelids too heavy to lift. She lifted them at last and

saw David's face. Tears of pity came into her eyes. Her voice had no sound.

He bent lower, and she whispered in his ear, "How —is—the—papoose?"

She wanted to make him smile. When he sobbed, she thought the baby was dead. The tears ran from her eyes. But David sobbed, "He's all right. Oh, Molly, Molly——"

The baby had been born on her seventeenth birthday, like a present. Molly noticed this when David was writing the baby's name and the date on the blank page for Births in their Bible. She hoped the baby would be like David, but she was glad he had been born on her own birthday.

They named him David John. He was a fat, healthy baby, and almost never cried. David teased him, tickled him, rumpled and tossed him, and he first laughed at sight of David. Molly washed his clothes every day and bathed him in snow water heated on the stove. When she sat holding him while he nursed, her happiness almost frightened her; it seemed too great to keep.

The snows went out with a rush that spring; the creek roared yellow and foaming to the door ledge. Then overnight the prairies were gay with wild flowers. The air was scented with violets, the plum trees bloomed. All day long the door stood open, and in the afternoons Molly took the baby and walked across the slough to the field where David was plowing.

The whole land was exuberant with change and

promise. Again the sky was clamorous with wild geese and ducks, but this year they did not stay to feed in the sloughs. They dropped down to rest, then flew on northward, for they saw the covered wagons and heard hammers and saws. That year the railroad tracks would be laid within ten miles of the homestead. Numbers of families were camped at the newest town site and frame buildings were going up. Lumber was still hauled from the East, but next year the trains would be running. Everywhere men were taking homesteads. Six miles, four miles, three miles away, there were dots of sod shanties on the prairie. Molly and David were glad they had come first and got the best homestead. All winter the tough sods had been rotting on their plowed land; now David plowed the fifty acres again and sowed wheat. They would have the first wheat in that country.

South of the town site a man was killed by claim jumpers who had taken his homestead while he was wintering in the East. The territory was not yet organized; there was no law. A posse pursued the claim jumpers, but they fled to the west and got away. If Molly had listened to that Mrs. Baker, the murdered man might have been David.

One morning in May, when the wheat field was green and David was planting potatoes in newly broken sod, a covered wagon drawn by oxen came slowly nearer across the prairie. That evening David showed Molly a camp fire half a mile away, just beyond the head of their creek, and next morning the strangers were building a sod shanty.

"We're going to have neighbors," David said, pleased.

Next morning he finished planting the sod potatoes, and walked the mile to welcome the newcomers. He came back bringing disappointment; they were Swedes, and could hardly speak English.

At dinnertime a few weeks later, Mr. Svenson appeared in the doorway. David sprang up and asked him in, but he shook his head. He stood on the threshold, a big man in dusty clothes, with calloused, helpless hands and a sorrowful, broad face, and his blue eyes glistened with tears. He stretched out his arm to the vast prairie; he made a sound like the ceaseless sound of the wind. He held up two fingers; one, he showed them, was himself, the other he left standing up alone. His wife. He held out his hands to Molly imploring, and the tears ran down his cheeks. His wife was lonely.

That afternoon Molly put on her best dress and bonnet, and taking the baby in her arms, she walked across the prairie. It was an adventure to go so far alone, under the enormous sky. There was no sound but the sound of the wind in the wild grasses. The Svensons' sod shanty was tiny in the immensity of earth and air. Beyond it a wisp of dust followed Mr. Svenson along a furrow. With the slow ox team, he was breaking sod.

Molly stood by the blanket that covered the shanty's doorway and shyly called, "Mrs. Svenson?"

A yellow-haired woman, no older than Molly, lifted the blanket and cried out. Trembling with joyous excitement, she led Molly by the hand into the shanty. The only chair was the wagon seat, taken from the wagon. Mrs. Svenson, eagerly smiling and talking incomprehensibly, urged Molly to sit upon it. Then, to Molly's surprise, she put coffee and water in the pot and hurried out to set it over a fire of buffalo chips in the open air. She had no stove.

The canvas wagon top lay folded on the floor, and on it a fat feather bed was neatly made up with fat pillows and counterpane. Barrels and boxes were neatly arranged in a corner. There were two large painted chests, and on the sod wall hung a picture of a cliff jutting into the sea. It was in a gold frame, and picture and frame were covered with pink mosquito netting to protect them from flyspecks.

Mrs. Svenson opened the chests and showed Molly her Swedish Bible and a Swedish-American grammar. She spread out embroidered cloths and a strange outlandish dress which Molly knew was her wedding dress, because she pointed to her ring. She covered one of the boxes with the prettiest cloth and set on it two cups and saucers, then brought in the coffee. Molly had never imagined such delicately thin cups; she could see the coffee through them. Mrs. Svenson was so anxious to please her that her hands trembled and little pleading looks darted from her eyes between her smiles.

"Cup and saucer," Molly said, pointing. Mrs. Svenson repeated, "Cup—and——" She laughed, shaking her yellow head. Her blue eyes squeezed to twinkles and all her strong white teeth showed. Molly liked her.

"Saucer," Molly said.

"Saucer," Mrs. Svenson said eagerly. Then she began pointing to other things. It was like a game. They were having a good time, laughing together.

"Ba-bee," Mrs. Svenson repeated many times, looking hungrily at the baby, and Molly let her hold him. He laughed and kicked in her arms; he seemed to like her too.

When Molly was leaving, Mrs. Svenson took her out by the sod barn to show her two hives of bees. Molly taught her "bees," and "honey," and she went home excited by so many things to tell David.

Sometimes twice a week, after that, Molly and Mrs. Svenson spent an afternoon together in the dugout or the shanty. They were company for each other. There were only men in the other sod shanties, and the women at the town site were ten miles away. The oxen could not go so far in a day, and the horses worked too hard in the fields to be driven for pleasure. But Molly felt that the country was settling up rapidly when she had a neighbor only about half a mile away.

There was really nothing more to wish for. The crops were thriving; there would be potatoes, turnips, carrots and flour for next winter, and money enough for other supplies. Next year, if all went well, they would have a cow. The year after that, there would be a calf. In less than five years, now, David would get the title to the land, and then they would build a frame house. They planned to build four rooms, and finish two at first.

They planted the seeds from the Lone Tree in a double row around the place they chose for the house. Every day when her other work was done, Molly lugged dozens of pails of water from the creek to the seedling cottonwoods. Some day they would be a tall windbreak around her home. When she bent over the tiny leaves and saw the water sinking into the thirsty earth, she felt a deep contentment.

One morning late in June she was startled at the washtub by a sudden darkening of the room. David was on the threshold. She knew something had happened.

"Come," he said abruptly. "I want to show you something." His voice shook with excitement.

She stripped the suds from her arms and dried her hands. David picked up the baby as heedlessly as if the baby were a bundle. He went up the path so quickly that Molly almost ran to keep up with him.

She saw nothing unusual. The wind was blowing, the wild grass rippling; no cloud was in the sky. The Svensons' sod shanty stood beside its shadow; dust followed Mr. Svenson's plow. Yellow specks of buildings were clustered at the town site and a smudge of dust blown against the skyline showed that men were working as usual on the railroad. David went with long strides toward the slough.

The coarse slough grass was taller than she; it rustled harshly along the narrow path. An earthy smell came from its roots, for here in the slough the creek spread and vanished in the soil, keeping it damp through the summer drought. She followed David out of the slough, and stood amazed. The wheat field's green stalks rose before her, breast high.

"Look. Molly, look!" David said, quivering. "Molly, look at it!"

It looked like a good crop, and she was glad.

"It's—in places it stands to my armpits," David said. "Of course, it's only in the milk yet——" His voice broke from control: "If it don't run forty bushels to the acre, I'll eat my hat!" he shouted.

"That's nice," she said.

"Nice!" he shouted. "You know what wheat's worth out here now? A dollar a bushel! This crop's worth two—thousand—dollars!"

The baby screamed. David let her take him, hardly aware of leaving him in her arms. "Look—look here!" he panted, seizing handfuls of the wheat stalks, measuring the heads against his finger. "Molly, look! Almost as long as my finger! And see how they're filling out! Every kernel! Two thousand dollars, I tell you, if it brings us a cent!"

She stood dazed, hushing the baby. Two thousand dollars—it was a sum outside reality. She couldn't imagine it. David had saved one hundred and six dollars, working on the railroad; they had been rich with all that money. Two thousand——

She said, awed, "Could we—we could have the cow."

"A cow!" David shouted. "A herd of cows! We'll fence the land. We'll build the house. I'm going to buy you a silk dress! We'll have a buggy and a driving team! Molly, you goose!" He seized her up in his arms and swung her around dizzily, prancing, whooping. "We're rich! Rich!"

"Goodness, David! Careful—the baby! David! Stop!"

He held her and the screeching baby still enclosed in his exuberant hug. His laughing, panting delight went all through her while they looked at the wheat. The wheat was real.

David had always been so much quicker than she. Slowly she came to share his feeling of liberation, of expansion, increasing as days went by. This puzzled her at first, for they had never been in want.

They had always been happy and comfortable, and the future had been bright. Yet now it was as if, chilled to the bone, they had come into a warm place.

Every evening they went to look at the wheat. They were silent, listening to the breathing of the myriad stalks in the wind. They gazed at the ripples of darker and lighter green passing over multitudes of bending heads.

Day by day the wheat was growing. No danger threatened it now; the time of frosts was past, it needed no more rain. Under the beneficent blaze of the sky the thin heads were growing plumper, the milky kernels swelling. To the very tip of all the long heads every husk was filling, day by day a little more crowding its fellows. David believed the yield would be even more than forty bushels to the acre. But Molly was prudent; she refused to think of more than two thousand dollars.

Inside the rows of tiny cottonwood seedlings David began to dig the cellar of the new house. He would have it built before the snows came. "We won't spend another winter in this hole in the ground!" he said. He despised the dugout now. Molly did not despise it; she forgot it in thinking of the new house.

In the evenings David figured the lumber he would need, while she pored over the lines he had drawn on paper. Here would be the kitchen, the pantry, the dining room, there the two bedrooms—two bedrooms!—and a parlor! She had been born in a log cabin, but David could faintly remember a white-painted house far in the East; this house was to be like that.

David's mind leaped into the next year, and the next:

"Next year, with the whole quarter section in wheat, we'll clear around five thousand dollars. By George, Horace Greeley knew what he was talking about!" He kindled like pitch pine catching flame: "Molly, we're in the West! We're growing up with the greatest country on earth! Five years from now we'll be riding high, wide and handsome!"

He thought that the homestead was not enough. "I ought to file on a tree claim."

"We'd have to set out a hundred trees and cultivate them five years," she said. "Haven't you got your hands full now? You'd work yourself to death, cultivating two quarter sections."

He laughed at her. "You little goose, what's money for? I'll hire help."

How simple! She hadn't thought of that. David was always opening wider vistas to her. He was right; they needed more land.

Before sunrise he was riding away in the wagon. A Land Office was at the town site now; he could drive the twenty miles and be home that night. Molly stood on the prairie above the dugout, holding the baby and watching until the wagon passed the slough.

There was treachery in the slough. The earth seemed dry and firm, but beneath it the dark water lay in the dark ground. There was a quivering when a wagon passed over it. The bog was there, hidden. It was harmless to horses walking confidently, and to wagon wheels that did not pause. The bog was dangerous only to those who trusted its deceiving surface, or who hesitated because they feared its unknown depths.

The wagon went out of sight in the tall slough grass. Only the seat moved smoothly forward like a boat floating, and David sat alert upon it. Slowly, he, too, sank out of sight. Molly thought of the bog.

Horses and wagon emerged on the low rise of ground beyond the wheat field. David was gazing at the wheat. He turned and waved his hat to her. The horses trotted onward and David and the wagon grew smaller until they vanished in the emptiness of the prairie.

The wind tugged at Molly's skirts. Already insects were shrilling to the sun's heat and grasshoppers leaped in the parching grass. Yet beneath heat and movement and sound she felt the infinite silence, in which no human voice would wake an echo.

The baby began to fret. His screwed-up little face, his toothless mouth wailing, the thrashing of weak fists and the violence of soft feet kicking, set the dimple quivering in her cheek. She held him close against the dissolving in her breast.

"There, there, mother's little man! Poor baby, he shall have a bath, he shall!"

The day's work was only a shell filled by a future more real to her than the present. At the new house there would be a well, with a pump; she would not carry water up the creek bank any more. The baby would have new clothes—soft flannel petticoats and sheer dresses trimmed with lace. There would be wooden floors, easily swept and mopped. She would do the washing in the big kitchen, where there would be plenty of room. There would be two large tubs, and when she wrung the clothes out of the suds, she'd drop them into the rinsing water; this would be so much easier than doing it all with one small tub. And suddenly she stopped, David's patched, sweat-faded shirt twisted between her hands, and her eyes widened at the thought, "We'll have so many clothes that I'll do the washing only once a week!"

A fiercer note in the sound of the wind alarmed her. The dugout was safe from a cyclone, but the wheat field—— From the doorway she could not see a cloud. The sky was a colorless vibration of heat and

the wind scorched her face. These hot winds, endless-
ly blowing, were ripening the wheat.

Stripped to his diaper, the baby slept on a cloth
spread on the floor for coolness. His skin was pale
and dewy, and there was something piteous in his de-
fenseless sleep, in the curled, tiny fingers and thin
neck. But his body was firm and sturdy; he was a
healthy baby. Before she weaned him, they would
have a cow.

That afternoon Mrs. Svenson came. Molly was
troubled by the indefinable change in their friendship.
There was an awkwardness between them. It made
no difference that the Svensons had only their few
acres of sod potatoes. But a difference was made,
even by their saying to themselves that there was no
difference.

Mrs. Svenson had brought her crocheting, and
Molly unfolded the handkerchief from the yards of
narrow lace she was knitting for the baby's new dresses. In the shelter of the dugout they sat working and
talking, so accustomed to the sound of the wind that
they did not hear it. Molly could not speak of the
new house without fearing the contrast with her
friend's poor little sod shanty. Yet not to speak of it
was to emphasize it by silence. If Mr. Svenson sowed
wheat next spring and had a good crop, they, too,
might have a frame house. But to say this seemed pa-
tronizing.

Eagerly Mrs. Svenson spoke of the wheat, of the
new house. Nodding, she repeated, "Iss goot, goot!"
She was assuring Molly that she was not envious. But

when she asked where David was, Molly could not say that he had gone to file on a tree claim. It meant that they would have twice as much land as the Svensons. She said, "He went to the town site."

A little silence fell, and they both spoke at once, to break it.

When Mrs. Svenson folded her crocheting and put on her bonnet, she asked, "You coom, my house?" Molly said too warmly, "Yes, yes, of course!"

A flush darkened Mrs. Svenson's tanned cheeks and she said, with dignity, "Goot, you coom, velcome." Molly's own cheeks burned.

From the top of the path she watched her friend trudging away, and felt a bewildered sense of loss. But she told herself when the new house was done, she would make Mrs. Svenson so warmly welcome in it, she would share so generously all her good fortune, that Mrs. Svenson would know that money could make no difference in their friendship.

The sun was setting, and faithfully she carried water to the seedling cottonwoods. Straightening her tired back, she looked at the raw hole in the earth that would be the cellar. She thought of the white house, sheltered by its windbreak of tall trees, surrounded by the fields pouring forth a wealth of wheat. Their home. The baby would never know any other. He would grow to boyhood and manhood in the big white house; he would work in the wheat fields and in the large barns; he would ride his own horse over the prairies. He would have no memory of a starved, poor life in a dugout.

The wind whipped her faded skirts. The rim of the sun, like a drop of dye, was spreading rosy color around the whole rim of the world. She lifted her face to the strong wind, and her expanding heart seemed to enclose the enormous land, the great sky, the whole West with its outpouring abundance of joy, of freedom.

It was dark when she heard the wagon and went to meet David at the barn with a lantern. The light fell on a load of lumber, and behind the wagon was a new, red mowing machine, its steel parts glittering. Packages were piled in the seat beside David.

He jumped over the wheel and seized her in a hug that drove the breath from her lungs. "Guess what I got for you!"

"But David,—— Oh, you didn't go in debt?"

"Why not? We're good for it, aren't we? This isn't a patch on what we're going to have! Say, you ought to hear 'em talking, in town, about our wheat! I filed a claim on the quarter section across the creek. We've got the best half section in this country! When it's all in wheat—— Golly, you didn't think I was driving that ten miles with an empty wagon? We've got to have the mowing machine, haven't we—and the lumber?"

She shared his excitement, admiring while he showed her the marvelous machine, with its levers that raised and lowered the sharp knives, and its iron seat on which a man could ride at ease while he was working. She patted the lumber and caught her breath when David pointed out four window sashes and tore the paper wrapping to show her the panes of real glass. He heaped her arms with packages—the soft one, she knew, was dress goods—and she exclaimed, "Oh, David, you shouldn't!" But he was looking at her eyes.

There had never been such a supper, such an evening. David had brought a beefsteak. He had brought candy and raisins, and even a pound of butter and a pound of white sugar. He had brought a rattle for the baby, and a tin horn, and a pair of little boots much too large for him now. And the soft package disclosed yards of shimmering brown silk. Molly gasped, incredulous. But it really was silk. She touched it reverently.

David put his arm around her and stroked her hair with his cheek. "Your hair's a lot silkier. I guess maybe I forgot to mention it, but you're pretty nice to have around. I'm kind of glad I've got you." He tried to speak lightly, but a cry burst from his heart: "Thank God, I'm going to be able to take care of you and the baby the—the way I ought to."

She had never doubted that. She hadn't guessed that under his gay confidence he had sometimes been frightened, afraid he might not be able to take care of wife and children as a man should. Now he wasn't ashamed to let her know it, because the fear was gone. He had proved what he could do in the West.

After supper was eaten, the baby nursed and put to sleep, they sat together in the doorway and looked at the stars. They were closer together, more married, than they had ever been. They did not think of the wheat, but they rested together in the security it had given them.

The air was still warm, but the fierceness of heat and wind had gone with the sun. A breeze moved over the grasses with a sound like the tranquil breathing of the sleeping earth. From the infinite height of the sky each large star hung suspended on an invisible thread. A kindness seemed to enclose earth and sky and all living things.

Next morning they went to look at the wheat. It was almost ripe. The long heads drooped with the weight of grain in the bearded husks, and golden-green lights and tawny shadows rippled across them. David looked long at the kernels in his palm and said reluctantly:

"We better give it another two weeks—maybe ten days. If this heat keeps up——"

There was no wind, the sky was growing pale before the terrible sun. Already the air began to waver in glassy sheets, and the flight of grasshoppers made a crackling sound in the prairie grasses, as though they were crisping in the heat.

In mid-morning David came from the field where he was breaking sod. "Whew!" he said. "Today's a scorcher! The horses couldn't stand it. I had to put 'em in the barn where there's shade. If this keeps up, I'll be cutting the wheat, end of next week."

He reached for the dipper in the water pail, and she said quickly, "You sit down and cool off; I'll get some fresh."

"Not so you'd notice it! What you got a hulking,

lazy husband around the house for?" Sweat stood out suddenly on his upper lip, a drop trickled down his cheek and the muscles of his neck glistened wet. He took off his hat and mopped forehead and neck with his handkerchief. "Golly, I can't wipe 'em dry. Outdoors it's too hot to sweat."

He went whistling for the water, came whistling back, and sat down to play with the baby. Molly was putting dinner on the table when they heard the scream. It came again and again—a woman's frantic screaming.

"You stay here," David said, clapping on his hat. He seized his gun and was gone. The baby kept on gurgling and kicking. Molly put on her sunbonnet. Outdoors the heat was dizzying. She went no farther from the baby than the top of the path.

The glassy air was moving upward in visible undulations. Its wavering broke the glinting reflections of the sky that lay in long streaks across the land.

Through glittering distortions Mrs. Svenson was coming, running, and David was running toward her. They approached each other swiftly. Mrs. Svenson cried out, panting, some word of warning and terror. She clutched her side, turned, and pointed upward. Molly saw the pointing hand change to a fist shaken at the sky.

A cloud was coming from the northwest, moving swiftly over the sun. It was a cloud like none that Molly had ever seen. She knew the piled darkness of thunderheads, the terrible green sky from which the cyclone dips and lifts and dips again its groping black tentacle. This was a cloud ineffably beautiful, soft as moonbeams, iridescent as mother-of-pearl. It covered the sun, and the sun shone through it gently, with kindness. The edge of the cloud moved onward swiftly, evenly. It moved above the windless prairie with the speed of wind.

Mrs. Svenson fell on her knees, sobbing, her apron over her head. She jumped up and ran sobbing toward her sod shanty. David took his gaze from the cloud to glance after her, and shook his head, puzzled. He stared upward again.

Molly thought there was a pattering like rain on the grass around her, but she could see only rustling blades and springing grasshoppers. David called to her, "Molly, what do you make of——"

She saw him stand as if frozen. He cried out, "Good—God—almighty!"

Grasshoppers were coming out of the sky, out of that cloud. They were dropping by dozens, by hundreds. The air twinkled with their shining wings, coming down. The cloud was grasshoppers.

David ran toward the barn, shouting, "The wheat! Fill the tub, soak blankets! Fire—maybe fire'll save it!"

And there remained not
any green thing

II

THE descent of the grasshoppers was, mercifully, a nightmare. It was a horror, but it was unbelievable. Some saving resistance in David and Molly refused to believe it. They refused to believe that they would not save the wheat.

The windless day encouraged them. They could control the fires they lighted. Surely the grasshoppers, with hundreds of miles of prairie before them, would avoid flames. Before the winged creatures had ceased to fall from the sky, David had driven the snorting, trembling horses thrice around the wheat field. Three furrows of upturned earth protected the wheat from the fire he set in the wild grass.

It was Molly's part to follow the fire along the strip of plowed ground, to keep the flames from crawling or leaping into the wheat. David had the harder task of fighting the fire in the grass. If it escaped him, the whole country would be burned over; nothing, then, could keep the grasshoppers out of the field. But there was no wind.

The fire ran merrily crackling, sending up waves of

fiercer heat into the heat of the sun. All the glassy air was in motion. Back and forth Molly ran, gasping, beating at wisps of burning grass, stamping them into the earth with her feet. For moments together she lost sight of David. The smoke came in gusts, stinging her eyes, her throat. With the smell of the clean smoke there was another, oilier smell; grasshoppers, caught by the licking heat, fell wingless into the fire. Their bodies burst with soft, popping sounds.

It seemed that this madness of fighting had never begun, would never end. There had never been and would never be anything but this fierce, relentless and desperate battle. Yet it ended. The last clump of burning grass smoldered on blackened ground.

Molly dissolved in trembling. Having nothing to lean against, she swayed and the firm earth held her. It was good to lie on.

David came striding to her and glanced quickly to see that she was all right. He was grimy with smoke, his eyelashes were gone and the hair was scorched from his arms.

"They don't seem to be eating anything," he said huskily, and coughed. "Maybe it was a false alarm."

Molly sat up, then got to her feet, steadying her knees. The wheat stood as before, golden-green and beautiful, with a whirring of grasshoppers over it.

"You go in and rest," David said. "I'm going to keep up a good thick smudge. That'll do the trick!"

She walked through grasshoppers thick as spray around her knees. They crunched sickeningly under her feet; she could not avoid stepping on them. Grasshoppers were in her hair, in her sleeves, in her skirts. Her ears tried to shut out the whirring of their wings.

Mechanically she cared for the baby. At the usual time she cooked supper. That night she fed the horses and led them to water. David was cutting slough grass and piling it on the burned strip around the wheat field. Thick smoke rose and spread in the motionless air.

Molly kept supper warm for a long time. At last she let it grow cold. She lay down without undressing and slept a little. David came in at last, too tired and restless to eat. He was angry when she urged him to rest.

"I'm not a baby! Losing a little sleep won't hurt me!" he said.

She went with him to the wheat field. In the starlight they stirred the heaps of smoldering grass, buried the flames under masses of dampened stalks, kept the heavy smoke pouring into the air.

Dawn came murky through the smoke hanging above the wheat field. When the sun's first rays struck across the prairie, a sound rose from it. It was a small, vast sound of innumerable tiny jaws nibbling, crunching. A trembling began in the wheat field. Tall stalks shivered; here and there one moved as if it were struggling. It swayed and leaned crookedly against its fellows.

David shouted hoarsely and plunged into the field. They had never gone into the wheat, not even to examine it, unwilling to break down one precious stalk. Now David trampled them down, he tore them up by armfuls, shouting, "Molly quick! Come help! Quick!"

Smudges placed thickly through the field might save some of it. David raved, "Fool! Fool! Why didn't I do this sooner?"

It was like tearing their own flesh, to tear up the roots of the wheat, to pile up heaps of the ripening grain and set fire to it. They worked in the smoke, in the heat, destroying the thing they wanted to save. A sacrifice of part might save the rest. They trampled down the thick stalks, they cleared spaces, they smothered the flames of burning wheat with the earth on its roots.

Through the smoke, David shouted, "Molly, you get out of this! Get back to the dugout and stay there!"

She went on working till he came to her. She said, "No, David, I——"

Coughing in the smoke, he croaked, "Get out, I tell you! What're we thinking of? You're nursing the baby!" Tears from his reddened eyes smeared the grime on his cheeks.

At the edge of the field she heard again that sound of nibbling. She stood and looked at the wheat. Scores of stalks were moving jerkily, as if they were struggling. The nibbling sound came from the whole prairie. It was not so loud as the flight of grasshoppers before her skirts, but it was continuous. It did not grow louder or softer; it did not stop. The prairie grasses had everywhere a restless movement, not made by any breeze. It sickened her to feel grasshoppers crushing to slime on the soles of her shoes.

The Svensons were burning smudges around their poor little field of sod potatoes and turnips.

Outside the door of the dugout she took off her shoes. In the doorway she took off her dress and petticoat and shook the grasshoppers out of them. The baby lay wailing in his cradle. She talked and sang to him while she bathed in the washbasin, then took him in her arms and lay down to rest. He cried hungrily. When she was cooler she let him nurse, and fanned him till he fell asleep. Then she fetched water from the creek and mixed a generous drink of vinegar, molasses and water to take to David.

He drank gratefully, draining the last drop from the little pail. It quivered in his hand. The nibbling sound was all around them, and looking into his bloodshot eyes, she found courage to say:

"David, you might as well rest. It's no——"

He shouted, "I'll save it or die trying! I'm not licked yet, not by a damn sight! My God, don't *you* turn against me!" He dashed the pail on the ground and left her as though he hated her.

Molly picked up the pail. Between the smudge fires, patches of the wheat were still standing. Their tops lay in ridges, like grass lodged by the wind. Each blade and every bearded head of grain quivered a little. Before Molly's eyes, one tall stalk fell, then another, and a hollow in the ridged tops slid lower. A whir of grasshoppers shot up from it.

What she feared was that David would be killed by sunstroke.

Every hour she carried a cool drink to him. She took him food, but he would not stop to eat. His wild look frightened her. She could not persuade him to leave the field where he was working in the heat, under the blazing sun. That evening she did the chores again, and went to the field determined to make David rest. He would not listen to her. But the sun was sinking at last.

The baby had the colic; she could not leave him again. She fed him peppermint water and patiently walked up and down, patting his little buttocks while he yelled on her shoulder. She carried him up the path and looked at smoke rising luridly in the starlight. Every step crushed the loathsome grasshoppers, and even in the night she could hear their nibbling.

Next morning the baby slept, exhausted. Molly took tea and bread to David. He drank thirstily and choked down a few mouthfuls of bread.

"We'll save some of it," he said, looking at the ravaged field. "Not much, but some. I figure near a tenth of it's still standing. They can't take all of it, you know. It isn't possible. Some of it's bound to be left. Enough for flour and seed. If we just have seed—— I can get time on those debts, if I put in a crop. I'll save enough for seed. If I just keep up this smudge."

Molly felt a little hope. If even a few stalks were left, here and there, she and David could gather each one carefully. They could live that winter on game and the sod potatoes, and put in another crop in the spring.

Then the rising sun struck her shoulders with its heat. Time did not seem to be passing; it stood still, quivering a little under the cruelty of the sun, trembling a little to the ceaseless, metallic nibbling.

That afternoon the grass was no longer standing on the prairie. It lay as if mowed, and still it was restlessly shaken. Bringing a pail of water from the creek, Molly halted and stared at the little plum trees. Not a leaf was left. She went into the dugout and set about mixing the vinegar and molasses for David's drink. The doorway behind her darkened. She was still an instant, then turned.

David's eyes were red in his sooty face. He straightened his shoulders and tried to speak robustly through a raw throat:

"Well, Molly, the jig's up. I—I can't——" His mouth twisted and he said brutally, "The wheat's gone. Every spear." He dropped heavily onto the bench.

Molly had known this would happen; she had known it when the first wheat stalk fell. She had known it when the nibbling began. Now it had happened, and something within her cried out that it could not be true.

"Why don't you say something?" David raged at her. And covered his face with his hands.

Molly turned away instantly. She mustn't let him break down.

"I guess if there isn't any wheat, we'll get along

44

without it," she said equably. "You've got along all
right without it so far."

But they had never been in debt before.

She measured the molasses, poured the vinegar,
stirred the mixture round and round. "I'm mixing up
some vinegar and water. You'd better wash up and
drink it while it's nice and cool."

To her surprise, she began to cry. Her mouth
writhed uncontrollably and tears ran from her eyes.
She went on stirring till she heard David at the washbasin, then she dried her face and blew her nose.

David wiped his blistered arms gingerly, ran the
comb through his wet hair, and drained the cup she
handed him. "Gosh, Molly, that hits the spot!"

"You're hot and tired," she answered. Even in the
dugout the maddening, ceaseless sound of nibbling
gnawed at their ears.

Tears brimmed his raw lids. He drew her against
him where he sat on the bench. She felt the sob shake
his body when he turned his face against her shoulder, and she knew that, as she had clung to him when
the baby was born, he was clinging to her in this misery too great to bear alone.

"There, there," she said. "It's all right. I was afraid
you'd get sunstroke. We're going to be all right."

"Oh, Molly, if I hadn't been such a fool! Those
debts I ran up—— How'll I ever pay—in debt almost two hundred dollars—— Not even flour for this
winter; not even seed."

"Never mind now. You'll manage all right. You're

tired; you're worn out. You'll feel better when you've had some sleep."

He slept heavily, exhausted. Next morning his face was creased and his eyes swollen. After he had done the chores and eaten breakfast, she persuaded him to lie down again. He fell asleep at once, and Molly sat quiet in order not to disturb him. Her head was heavy and she let it sink against her arm on the table. Dozing, she was all the time aware of David in the bunk, of the baby on the floor. Her eyes opened and she saw the baby absorbed in his own pink feet. He frowned intently, staring with slightly crossed eyes at the inexplicable things wavering about him, and patiently he tried to lay hold of the toes that eluded his uncertain grasp.

Suddenly Molly was aware of a new sound—a rasping, clicking, scratching sound. It crawled up her spine and over her scalp. She started to her feet, and saw the top of the door jamb rippling like a snake. The clean black line was scaly, and rippling, pouring inward.

She snatched up the baby, wrapped him in her apron, covered him with her arms. Then she saw the thing clearly. The grasshoppers were coming into the dugout. The ridged long backs jostled one another. Hundreds, thousands of hard, triangular heads, knobbed with eyes, pointed with nibbling jaws, were coming downward, turning, moving inward over the door jamb.

She screamed.

The door stood open against the creek bank. She

seized the latch. An instant she saw the whole earth crawling—path, creek banks, prairie, scaly and crawling. The door closed horribly, crunching grasshoppers. "David!"

He seized her. "Molly, what—— You're sick!"

Her teeth were chattering.

She screamed, "No, no! Kill them! Kill them!" In the dark she could hear them crawling.

David lighted the lamp. She stood trembling while he killed them. He brushed them from ceiling and walls, crushed them with his boots, hunted them out of the hay box and the stove. He shook them out of the bedding and swept them from beneath the bunk. He looked into the water pail.

"Throw it out" she cried.

"I don't know—— You want me to get more?"

"No, no don't open the door! I'll boil it!"

He skimmed them out of the water with the dipper.

She was ashamed to be behaving so, and with an effort she ceased to tremble and relaxed her clenched jaws. Then the baby screamed, a sharp yell of pain. Molly quickly uncovered him on her lap. From his soft armpit a grasshopper leaped, struck her cheek, stirred its claws there and crawled. She struck it away and began to cry loudly, like a child. For a time she could not stop crying, even in David's arms. When she was quiet, they heard the grasshoppers crawling on the paper windowpane. Grasshoppers were a mottled shadow crawling steadily downward across it, and by that they knew that the whole earth was still crawling in the sunlight outside.

All that night the creatures crawled, and all the next day. David slipped out to take care of the horses. When he came back, Molly did not ask him any questions. They sat all day in the dugout behind the closed door.

"The railroad's left," David said. "This won't stop the railroad. I'll go back to work on it for a while. Oh, we're not licked yet by a long ways! We'll make out all right."

"Of course we will," Molly said. "We always have."

She knew how he hated to go back to work on the railroad. It had been different when they were starting out. Now for a year he had had his own land; he had been independent. It was hard to go back obeying other men's orders for wages. But it couldn't be helped. When they were silent, they could hear the claws on the paper pane.

Later that afternoon the oiled paper shone clear. David opened the door.

As mysteriously as they had come, the grasshoppers were going. They had ceased to crawl, they had left the ground. A translucent cloud, colored like mother-of-pearl, swept northwestward across the sun.

The prairie was bald earth, not a blade of grass remained. Dust blew in the evening breeze. A faint stench rose from the creek. The water was solidly filled with drowned grasshoppers, rotting. No more clean water remained in all that country.

"I didn't want to worry you," David said, "but the horses haven't had water since yesterday morning. They've been two days without water in this heat. Creek was full of grasshoppers when I went out yesterday."

Long after sunset he worked, digging a hole in the slough. Mr. Svenson came, carrying a shovel and a pail and leading his oxen. They worked together, digging. When the hole was deep enough, they had to wait for water to seep into it.

At midnight the horses and the oxen drank, and Mr. Svenson started home with the pail full of water. Molly was lying awake when David came in, mud-stained and cheerful. She sat up eagerly to drink from the brimming dipper he gave her.

"Thank God the horses are all right," he said. "I'll be sure to get a job with the teams."

There had been no use trying to dig a well while the grasshoppers were crawling. "Nothing stopped them," he told Molly while he took off his boots. "No matter what they came to, they went right on. They were crawling up one side of the barn and down the other. Crawling west. They crawled straight into the creek, never stopped. They crawled into it and drowned till they clogged it up and the others crawled across on their backs. Molly——" He hesitated. "I wish you'd seen it. A thing like that. It was—— They had some idea, or—— Would they do a thing like that without knowing why? I tell you they were bound to go west. All the power of hell couldn't've stopped them."

He and Molly looked at each other for a long moment. She asked, "You don't think——"

"What?" he asked at last.

Neither of them could say what they felt. The grasshoppers—crawling into the creek and drowning till the others crossed on their backs. Grasshoppers, going west—like the railroads, like the people, like cities and settled lands and law and government. Yet grasshoppers were as alien, as indifferent to human suffering, as wind or cold. Perhaps they were no more indifferent to human beings than human fate itself.

"Well, it's good the horses were saved," Molly said. "We better go to sleep if you're getting up early."

He drove away next morning before daylight. The nearest railroad camp was twenty miles away and he said cheerfully that he'd waste no time getting there.

"If I get a job," he said—"I mean if the foreman puts me to work right away—I'll stay with it. I'll try to find a rider coming this way and send you word, but don't be worried if I don't get home tomorrow night."

"No," she said.

"Svenson'll kind of look out for you. He told me he'd be glad to."

"Yes," she said.

He held her close for a minute, by the wagon wheel in the lantern light. Then he kissed her. She held up the baby, and David tickled a gurgle from him. "Be good, little shaver. Take care of your mother."

He climbed to the wagon seat, picked up the reins and drove away. In a little while she heard a whistled tune growning fainter across the dark prairie. She knew he was whistling to cheer her.

IN THE daylight she saw the devastated country more clearly. There was nothing but bare earth to the rim of the sky. Earth, and a little litter of old, dead weed stalks. The grasshoppers had not eaten the stacks of slough hay left from last year. They and the barn stood gaunt above their shadows on the shadowless prairie. All the naked earth was pitted by the little holes where the grasshoppers had left their eggs. Grasshoppers would be bad next year, but crops could survive them; David had told her that.

She fetched water from the hole in the slough to bathe the baby and wash his clothes and hers. Nothing would remove the brown spots left by the grasshoppers. The muddy water must settle before she drank it; it was lukewarm. She would have made hot tea for herself, but there were so few tea leaves. The stench from the creek grew stronger in the heat. Dust blew across the grassless prairie; everything she touched was gritty with dust. The slough grass was gone, like the rest, and when, at sunset, she carried the baby up on the prairie to escape the smell of the creek, she saw a little strawy stubble in the wheat field, between the blackened patches where the smudges had burned. The seedling cottonwoods were dead, of course; they were tender twigs and leaves; the grasshoppers had eaten them.

She did not know how anxious she was, until the strain eased on the second night. David did not come. She told herself that she had been sure he would get a job. Now they could pay something on the debts and buy supplies for next winter and seed for next year. He would need the mowing machine, and some day no doubt they would use the lumber and the windows. Only the brown silk had been a serious mistake, but she could not really regret that David had bought it for her.

Late that night David had not come, and she fell asleep in a great sense of safety. In the morning she felt rested and strong. The days since the grasshoppers came had been a delirium; now it was gone. The stench from the creek would be gone, too, in time, and grass would grow again in the spring. She told herself that the loss of the wheat was not a real loss; they had never harvested the grain, they had never had the new house, the pump, the two washtubs, the driving team and buggy. None of these had been real.

Yet when she struggled with the broken lid on the old stove, she felt defrauded of her new stove. Dipping water from the hole in the slough and carrying it all the long way across the prairie and down the path, she rebelled against the loss of her pump. She could have wept over the baby's thin, pieced petticoat; over the soft, sweet new flannels and the dresses trimmed with lace that had been taken from him; and the thought of the cow was a poisoned stab.

"David has a job," she said to herself. "We will have a cow next year." She need not be afraid; little David John would have milk.

"Yes, he shall; so he shall, mother's baby," she crooned to him, glad because his wandering fist tugged sharply at her smooth hair. But the angry sense of injustice welled up again. She hated the dugout—"hole in the ground," as David had said—she hated the broken stove, the heat, the stripped, ugly prairie. She hated the wind that rasped her nerves and covered everything with dust. Her whole life seemed poor and mean. Fiercely, bitterly, she pitied her defrauded baby. She pitied David, robbed, hurt, forced to work for other men. Her loneliness rebelled against the cruelty that took him from her. They did not deserve this suffering. They had trusted, and been betrayed. Her cry was, "It isn't right! It isn't fair!"

She laid the sleeping baby on the floor and barricaded the doorway with the bench. Taking the hoe and a bushel basket, she went through the hot and dusty winds to the field where David had planted potatoes in newly broken sod. The potato tops were gone, but part of a crop remained buried in the parched earth. Carefully she dug and carefully sifted the earth with her fingers, so as to lose not the smallest potato.

The Svensons were digging their potatoes too. Moving shadows led the eye to their earth-colored figures, trudging and stooping in a dust mist. The sky was copper colored; no longer infinitely vibrating, it seemed to clang to the blows of the sun's heat.

Late that afternoon Molly fetched water from the slough and wearily bathed. She fed the baby and dressed him in his poor shirt and petticoat and faded calico dress, and carrying him against her shoulder, she walked to the Svensons'. She felt that talking with her friend would ease her bitterness.

In the stifling shanty, Mrs. Svenson, with gestures and halting words, eagerly described their fight against the grasshoppers. She told how the bees had poured from their hives to attack the crawling hordes. She lamented the garden, but some turnips and carrots remained, and the potatoes. Her narrow eyes sparkled and her teeth gleamed in her grimy face. She could not wash; only a little water remained in the pail, and there would be no more till Mr. Svenson hauled it from the hole in the slough.

"Iss no goot! Iss bad, bad! So! Ve make out, yes?" She patted Molly's hand.

Molly thought the Svensons had not lost a great deal. They had their sod potatoes, turnips and carrots, and their bees. They wouldn't have had much more if the grasshoppers had not come. And they were together; they were not separated. They were not in debt. Molly's sense of her own loss did not grow less bitter.

She told how David, with his own hands, had uprooted and burned their wheat, desperately trying to save only a little of it. But it was gone. Nothing, nothing was left. She found herself cherishing the greatness of their loss, as though the loss itself were a possession. Her tongue, as if by its own volition, dwelt upon every detail of their misery. It seemed to brag about what they had lost. Molly could not stop it. She did not understand herself. Her bitterness was like a poison, like a fever that had taken possession of her.

Suddenly she was tired, exhausted. She wanted David. Nothing was right without him. Only part of herself was left when he was gone, and her longing for him was more than she could bear. Tears came into the corners of her eyes; she turned her head and winked them away. Mrs. Svenson's hand took hers, and Molly clung to it.

When Mr. Svenson stopped the ox team by the door, Molly gave her friend the baby to hold while she climbed into the wagon. They leaned toward each other and for the first time they kissed.

"Yes, yes," Mrs. Svenson said, nodding her bright head. "You coom, I coom, ve—— Like this, we make out!"

The oxen drew the wagon slowly across the prairie. Behind the seat the empty pail and tub jangled together. Mr. Svenson shook his head, sighing deeply; without his oxen he would have nothing, he would be helpless, and he did not know how he could feed them; there was no wild hay.

The sunset had never been so gorgeous. Great banners of crimson, rose and orange unfurled to the zenith. Their reflections colored the air and land, and the putrid water in the creek glowed like jewels. Molly thought of David, far away. She tried not to think of all the empty days she must endure till winter, when he could come home.

He came five nights later. Molly was nursing the baby when she heard the wagon. His mouth lost her breast and he complained angrily. She laid him squalling on the bunk and went outdoors to listen. It was David's wagon, stopping by the barn.

The baby screamed while she lighted the lantern; she left him howling with rage. There was a sickle moon, and when her head rose above the creek bank she saw the dark shapes of wagon and drooping horses, and David hunched on the seat.

The lantern light showed dust thick in the hollows of his eyes and in the lines around his mouth. It showed the endless miles he had traveled that day in dust and heat, alone, defeated. The jolting of the wagon had pounded all day long on mind and body, the sky and the prairie had mocked him.

"Here I am," he said bitterly.

"You must be tired out." Her voiced caressed him. "I'll help unhitch."

"I can't get a job."

She had known that when she heard the wagon. She said, "Well, you're here!"

He climbed stiffly down over the wheel. Dust slid out of the folds of his sleeve when she laid her hand on his arm. She held up her face, and he kissed her briefly and turned away to unfasten the traces.

Molly knew what he felt: a man had no right to a wife he couldn't take care of. She was frightened; she didn't know how to reach him. Nothing else mattered, if only she and David were close together. He was there, he had kissed her, and he hadn't come back to her.

She looped up a dusty rein and blindly thrust the loops through the ring on the horse's collar. Her hands shook. She was trembling, lost, alone.

"You run along!" David said brusquely. "I guess I'm not so beat out that I can't manage to unhitch my own team!"

He was on the edge of collapse.

"All right," she said quickly. "I'll go put the teakettle on."

She tried not to feel so terrified, so forlorn. There was new bread for supper; she had baked a loaf that day. The small potatoes would boil quickly in their skins. She was glad she had not used the tea leaves; a cup of strong tea would make David feel better.

He did not hurry with the chores. There was time to finish nursing the baby and to make herself tidy. She filled the washbasin with fresh water and hung up a clean towel. The tea was boiling and the potatoes steaming dry when he came in.

His mouth and jaw had a new, hard look, and Molly was surprised by the thought, "Why, he's only twenty years old."

He looked older than ever before, and it was strange that she should think of him as young.

They did not talk much while he ate. He did not say anything about the baby. She spoke of the potato crop and the Svensons, and refilled his cup. Every word and every little sound was loud but helpless against a dreadful silence. All the time she was crying to him silently, "David, David, come back to me! Don't stay so far away!"

He pushed back the teacup and plate, and folded his arms on the edge of the table. His mouth hardened. "There isn't a job in the whole country."

Molly did not say anything. She knew, if there had been a job, David would have got it. She was desolate because he wouldn't come to her for comfort, he didn't want her mothering love.

"They're turning away men at all the camps," he went on. "You don't know what it's like." She saw his brown hands grip hard on his arms. "Everybody's looking for work. Half the folks at the town site are quitting, getting out. They've stopped building. They're shutting up the stores. At the railroad camps it's—— They're—Molly, they're begging! They're begging at the cook shanties. Men with families, babies—— They come along and—they have to beg for handouts."

"Why don't they live on jack rabbits?" Molly asked sharply.

"There aren't any. The jack rabbits have left the country. All the way east, sixty, or some say a hundred miles, the grasshoppers took everything. Molly, you don't understand. If you'd seen—— There was a man talking to me. He had a homestead south of Lone Tree; he'd built a frame shanty on it. He had three children in the wagon, and his wife is going to have another. And his horses—he couldn't feed them. He was going to drive them as far as he could—and when they couldn't go any farther, what could he do? Molly, he—while he was talking to me, he—broke down and cried."

She shut her mind to it. Nothing mattered but David. "That hasn't anything to do with us," she said. "We aren't going to beg."

"Oh, aren't we?" The words were cruel. They were like a blow. They broke something. "I'll let you and the baby starve, will I? It's sixty miles, I tell you—or a hundred, two hundred! And then God knows if I'll get work! Beg! Of course I'd beg! What do you think I'm made of?"

She had steadied herself, and said quietly, "No, David. It's not that bad. There's slough hay for the horses, and we have potatoes, and this winter you can hunt."

"Stay here, you mean? We'd have to have flour, and salt, and—even if we could get along without sugar—— Oh, my God, and you nursing the baby!"

He struck the table with his fist. "And I can't even hunt! I haven't the powder and shot, and my credit's no good!"

Molly had seized the lamp. The flame smeared soot on the glass chimney. David pressed his fists to his temples.

"No. We've got to give up the homestead and get out—if we can. Maybe I can get work if we can get far enough east."

"Give up the—— Oh, no!"

"Yes, give up the homestead!" He turned on her savagely. Molly knew he didn't mean it; he was not angry with her. "And I'll be lucky if I can steal—

that's what I said, steal!—steal my horses to get out with. Oh, you got a fine husband when you married me!"

"David, don't——"

"It's my fault. It's those damn debts. I tell you I'm licked. I'm—I tried everything. All the camps. Took sixty extra miles out of the horses, just on the chance—— Coming back, Loftus stopped me at the town site. Said I had to pay him for that lumber. I tried to get him to take it back; he wouldn't. He said if I tried to skip out without paying, he'd attach the team and wagon."

"He can't!" Molly cried. "He couldn't! Why, they hang horse thieves! It's murder—leaving a man on foot——"

"Oh, yes, he can. Yes, he will. There's law at the town site now. And I—— He as good as called me a thief, and I didn't do anything. I told him I'd give him furs on account, this winter. He agreed to that. Then I went to see Henderson about getting powder and shot, and he said he was sorry—sorry! I wasn't asking for any damn charity! He wouldn't give me another cent of credit. Nothing to live on. You and the little shaver—all winter—and no seed for next year——"

Molly was afraid to speak and afraid to let him hear his own breath shaking in the silence. If he broke down, he'd hate himself. If his pride went completely, there would be nothing left.

Suddenly she was almost happy, because she understood why he hadn't come to her for comfort. It was his pride—his pride in taking care of her and the baby. She would love him just as much if he couldn't take care of her. But she wouldn't love him at all without that pride; he wouldn't be David without it. That was why he had to save it; that was why he fought for it even against her. He must not lose his pride; it was their most precious possession.

She knew they must not give up the homestead. For an instant she wanted again the happy days when they had traveled together in the wagon, light-hearted and free.

But everything was changed now. Then they had been young, and going west. Only a defeated man traveled eastward, homeless, with a wife and little baby. All day long poor little David John, hot and tired and wailing, would be jolting in the wagon. All the way David would know, and every man he met would know, that he hadn't been strong enough for the West.

"Why don't you just go east till winter?" she said. "Don't give up the homestead. Henderson and Loftus will give us time on the debts if we hold on to the homestead."

"How can we make a trip like that and get back inside five months?" he answered dully. "We'll have to travel slow with the baby, and we've got to live. Somebody'll jump the place as soon as we're gone, anyhow. A fine place like this—all the plowed land——"

He had not even thought of going east without her. "Nobody'll jump it while I'm here," she said stoutly.

He understood then, looking up quickly, looking into her eyes. "Molly, you don't mean you'd——"

"I'm just as lonesome when you aren't here, no matter where you are. If you were working on the railroad or in the East." She would not let her voice tremble. Hurriedly she ended, "I'll be all right. The Svensons are here."

He came swiftly and gathered her up in his arms. "Molly, sweetheart! My poor dear. Did you miss me so much?"

"Yes," she said. He was trembling and tears came into his eyes, as though he had not known how much she missed him.

"I won't leave you," he said. "I won't ever leave you any more. We'll stick together, no matter what happens. That's all that matters."

"Of course," she said. But she knew he must go. She marveled that a man's pride was so essential to him that he could not let it go and be content with love. But that was true. If David's pride were hurt to death, they would really lose each other forever, as she had lost him all those wretched hours.

That night they lay talking while the baby slept cozily between them, and she was able to make him see that it was quite simple; he could be working in the East instead of on the railroad. That was all.

THEY had two days together before he went away. She helped him dig the rest of the potatoes and the turnips. He deepened the well in the slough and set a windlass above it, so that she could draw a full pail of

clear water. The second evening they spent at the
Svensons', and walked slowly homeward together in
the moonlight, the baby asleep on his shoulder.

Next morning, with the lumber and window frames
on the wagon, he drove to the town site. It was cruel
that Molly could not go with him, but she dared not
take the baby so far in the heat. That night David
came back triumphant, with flour, salt, molasses,
kerosene, and even a piece of salt pork and two
pounds of tea. He had traded the lumber and windows for these supplies—enough to provide for Molly till he came back in the fall.

"And, Molly, you'd never guess!" he said, grin-
ning. "Loftus attached the team!"

"Oh, David——"

"Wait till you hear. Just as I was pulling out of
town, here came the sheriff with the paper. He said
he hated like the devil to take a man's team, but he'd
have to do it unless I squared the bill with Loftus.
Well, I told him how it is, and that sheriff's a good
fellow. Had to take the team, he said, but the attach-
ment didn't apply to my load, and he couldn't let me
dump it in the street—that being against city ordi-
nance. He said I'd better haul those supplies wherever they were going, and come back with the team.
Kind of winked when he said it. He thinks he's giving
us a chance to get out of this country between two
days. He's going to be a surprised man tomorrow
morning. And so's Loftus.

"Because, Molly, think. Loftus has to take the
team, and he can't get rid of 'em as a gift, the price

feed is now. He'll feed them till fall, and when I come back he'll be facing feeding them all winter. Why, he'll jump at a chance to get them off his hands. I bet I get 'em back for cost of the feed he's put into them. How's that for a joke?"

He hugged her jubilantly and they laughed together. They laughed a great deal that evening, trying to forget that David was leaving tomorrow. When they spoke of that, they spoke cheerfully. David would travel fast; when he reached railroad trains, he would beat his way on them. Crops were said to be good in the East; he would easily get work in the harvest. In the fall he would come back with plenty of money. They would have another cozy winter together, and then there would be spring again, a new year, a new crop.

To the very last, they were cheerful. Their smiles were shaky, but they smiled. David turned to wave his hat from the rise beyond the slough, and Molly held up the baby and flopped his little fist. She listened till silence closed down behind the wagon.

Day after day the sun rose and declined in the burning copper sky. Whirlpools of dust appeared and scurried and vanished. There were violently colored sunsets. Purple-black streaks of thunderstorm moved above the prairie, crackling and rumbling and dropping gray curtains of rain. Where they had passed, the unconquerable sod sent up its green blades. The grass in the slough grew shoe-top high and swished against Molly's skirts when she went to the well. But for Molly time itself stood still, waiting.

At night she dreamed horrible dreams. She had not told David how she feared trains. When she slept she saw the monstrous, inhuman things of steam and iron, swiftly coming, roaring, panting, staring with the headlights like eyes; things that seemed alive, but were not alive. She saw David spring forward, confident, valiant for her and the baby. She saw the trains killing him.

In the daytime she would not think of trains. She was waiting.

She had three spools of thread and her small steel knitting needles. When everything in the dugout was washed, scoured, patched, polished, when she could find nothing more to do, she knitted. She knitted up all the thread and unraveled the lace so she could knit it again. Often Mrs. Svenson was with her, and they talked, but Molly was always waiting.

Poor little David John was cutting teeth. His little gums were swollen and hot, and nothing could help him. He lay whimpering, pitifully turning from side to side, till he wailed because he could find no escape from misery.

Molly watched for riders on the prairie. All the shanties but the Svensons' had been deserted since the grasshoppers came, and few riders passed that way. When she saw one loping toward the south, she called, she shrieked, she ran. Panting, one hand against her side, the other shading her eyes, she looked up at the strange man in the saddle.

"Are you going to the town site? If you are coming

back this way, would you ask if there's a letter at the post office for me?"

A man with narrow eyes in wrinkled eyelids, a scar across a leathery cheek, two guns on his thighs. A frank boy, smiling with a white flash of teeth. A black-eyed halfbreed, bareheaded, riding a bare-backed Indian pony. They all said:

"Why, yes, ma'am, be glad to." But they did not come back.

Molly was sure there must be a letter at the post office—if nothing had happened to David.

Mr. Svenson was kind. The trip to the post office and back was a two days' journey for oxen or for a man on foot, but Mr. Svenson offered to go. Starting at twilight and walking all night, he could reach shade at the town site before the heat of next day. Molly set herself to wait only two nights and two days more. Then she would know.

That very afternoon she heard a horse's hoofs on the dugout; she heard a call. The scarred man sat on his horse beside the chimney. He had brought a letter.

Afterward Molly hoped she had properly thanked him. She remembered, afterward, that he had wheeled his horse and galloped away to the southeast; he must have come miles out of his way.

The letter was from Iowa.

Dear Wife: I take my pen in hand to let you know that I am well and hope you are the same. How are you and the little shaver? Are you getting along all right? I have

66

a job working at Roslyn Feed Mill, $30. a month and
board. Let me know how you are. Roslyn treats me fine,
he is all wool and a yard wide. Write me at this address
and let me know how you are getting along. I will be
home in Oct. I hope everything is all right there. Let me
know. Well so no more at this time from

Your Loving Husband
xxxxxxxx for you and the little chap

Molly wore the paper limp with reading it, long
after the words would repeat themselves to her. They
eased a little the strain of waiting for October. "Dear
Wife . . . Your Loving Husband. xxxx for you and
the little chap."

Mr. Svenson walked to town to mail her reply. He
was so kind that Molly felt she could never repay
him. She decided to let him cut the slough hay for her
on shares. She could have cut it herself, a little by a
little, resting in the heat of the day. But Mr. Svenson
needed the hay for his oxen, and David and she
would have enough, with the two stacks left from last
year and half the small new crop.

All one week Mr. Svenson was cutting, raking and
stacking the hay. Mrs. Svenson came with him every
morning, always bringing some part of the dinner,
and all three ate together at noon in the shady dugout. That week would have been a pleasure to be remembered, but for Mr. Svenson's gloom. The hay,
with some of his turnips, would winter the oxen
through, yet still he shook his head and muttered.

Molly thought at first that he was poor spirited.

But when he attacked the whole country, the West, she was angry.

"Ta tam country," he said. "No tam goot."

"The country's all right, Mr. Svenson," Molly said. Suddenly she felt that he was a foreigner; no American would talk like that. She said sharply, "No country's going to feed you with a spoon."

Mr. Svenson lifted his big fist and pointed with his knife to the vista beyond the doorway. The prairie was lost in heat; there was no horizon. Undulating air poured upward from all the wavering land. Dust devils were whirling, scurrying, leaping. Distances were shaken and the eye could not rest.

"Ta tam country, she feed nobody," Mr. Svenson said bitterly. "She iss devils, ta country."

Molly was silent. In politeness she could not say, "It's men that make a country. What's the matter with you?"

After a moment she said gently, "It's hot because there are no trees. But where there are trees, you have to cut them down and burn them, and dig out the stumps and sprout the fields. You have to fight the woods all the time. Out here in the West we'll plant the trees we want. It will be cooler when the trees are grown and all the land is in crops. It's good land."

She was thinking of David, who would come home in October. They had not lost the tree claim. If all went well, they would set out the little trees on it in the spring.

In September the summer heat was gone. The prairie stretched firm again to the sky's rim. Overhead the first long lines of wild birds were flying south. Molly was counting weeks now; only eight weeks, or seven, were between her and David.

One morning Mr. Svenson came down the path to the dugout and stood in the door. He spread out his calloused hands and let them fall lax. "Ve go."

"Go?" Molly asked. But she knew. The Svensons were giving up; they were going east.

Mr. Svenson struggled for words. Tears came into his eyes, as they had come when he told Molly that his wife was lonely. "Ta bee—little, little bee—big bee kill. Dead, all dead."

His bees were killing their broods. They were stinging to death the young bees, because they could not feed them through the winter. The grasshoppers had killed all the plants; the bees could find no blossoms from which to make honey.

Tears for the murdered little bees trickled down into Mr. Svenson's sunbleached beard. Passionately he said that he would not stay in a country where not even a bee could live. "Vork, vork, all time vork! No goot, no eat! Ve go!"

Molly was a little frightened when Mr. Svenson had gone on to water his oxen at the well. She had not known how much a part of her life the Svensons had become. Their going made her feel insecure. All summer she had kept the feeling that the country was settling up rapidly, when neighbors were only half a mile apart. The other sod shanties had been deserted since the grasshoppers came, but she had not felt their emptiness before.

She left her washing in the tub and hurriedly dressed little David John, thinking how David would grin to see the wave of hair on top of his head and the triumphant tooth in his moist smile. She put on her sunbonnet and walked across the prairie to see Mrs. Svenson.

Mrs. Svenson talked cheerfully about the East. She had a brother in Minnesota; they would go to him. That winter they would be in a crowded household in a country of roads and fenced fields and neighbors. There would be wood for the fires, and wood ashes for making soap; there would be milk and cream and butter. People would come and go; there would be gossip, jokes, sleighbells ringing through the woods on the way to dances. Mrs. Svenson talked of all these things and was very busy getting ready to go.

Only once, without meaning to, her eyes confessed the truth, and quickly Molly looked away. Mrs. Svenson knew that her husband was giving up, that he would be only a hired man in the East. But she smiled, tossed her head with its yellow braids, and said, "Ve coom back! Iss plenty land, yes?"

Yes. But David would own his land in four years more. David would never give up, with no more reason than Mr. Svenson had. It was not only this quarter section of land that Mr. Svenson was giving up; it was a year of his life, a year's work and hope. Molly doubted that Mr. Svenson would ever be more than a hired man.

He began hauling his potatoes and turnips and his share of the slough hay to the town site and trading them for supplies they would need on the trip. Even his plow went into the trade for powder and shot, for wood for wagon bows, and grain to feed the oxen. One day he trudged the ten miles beside the nigh ox, the next day he rode back. Mrs. Svenson mended the canvas wagon top and baked hard-tack for the journey.

Mr. Svenson set out on his last trip to town. When he returned, they would be all ready to leave as soon as David came.

The next evening at sunset, Molly heard him call. She ran up the path to the prairie. He was unfastening the oxen from the wagon as usual; because of the treachery in the slough, he drove the wagon across it, then led the oxen back to the well to drink. He paused, and fumbling in his blouse, took out a letter. His broad face beamed with pleasure in Molly's joy. The letter would say when David was coming.

Quickly and carefully she slit the envelope with a hairpin and took out the folded sheet. Two limp bank notes lay in it. Her heart stopped, and started with a jerk that shook the paper. She could hardly hold it still enough to read the words on it.

Dear Wife: I take my pen in hand to let you know do not worry. I have met with an accident but am getting along fine. Molly I cannot get home in Oct. My leg is broke in two places and ankle hurt but the doc says I am mending fast. He says I am in fine shape. I will not be lame. I have your dear letter and am glad you are well

and the little shaver fat and sassy. Molly you better
make arrangements to stay with Svensons. I do not
know when I can travel and it is liable to be a bad winter there. Game will be scarce. Wolves and outlaws will
be moving back to settled country. Stay with Svensons
and he will take care of you. Have him build you a
shanty joining his. I send what money I can for supplies.
Molly you and the baby will be safe with Svensons
and I will come as soon as I can. Now do not worry
about me. Roslyn is the whitest man I know. We were
moving his feed mill and he could not hold up the heft
and let it fall on me. It was not his fault but he claims it
was. He is not charging me a cent for board while I am
laid up and even says he will pay the doc. The way he
puts it I feel all right to let him and he is so rich he will
not miss it. So do not worry, I am all right. Move to
Svensons' and get settled before cold weather. Molly,
dear Wife, do the best you can. Try not to miss me the
way I miss you. I am never going to leave you again as
long as we live. Write to me.

Your Loving Husband

Mr. Svenson came from the slough, leading the
oxen. He looked expectantly at Molly. All his potatoes and hay were gone now, and he and his wife
were ready to leave. They were waiting only until
David came. Every day was precious, for they must
begin the long journey soon in order to reach North-
ern Minnesota before the heavy snows fell.

Mr. Svenson's pleased expectancy changed to dis-
may when he saw Molly's face. She was not trembling now. Her fingers, cold and steady, folded the
letter. David was alive; thank God, his life had been

spared. She had never realized before that David might die. She might never see him again.

"He isn't coming," she said. "He's been hurt." Even those words did not pierce her numbness. Only a little part of her was alive, and it was numb and firm as a rock. She must decide what to do. Her eyes were looking at the bank notes; with attention they followed the lines of the engraving. Two ten-dollar bills; two times ten is twenty.

She must decide what to do; all the responsibility was now hers. A corner of one bill was turned down. She straightened it and carefully smoothed out the creases. With no effort to reason or choose, she said, "I must take the baby and go to the town site."

In a little old sod shanty
on a claim

III

AFTERWARD Molly remembered the day at the town site as though it had happened to someone else. Even at the time everything had an air of unreality, perhaps because she was so tired.

She was ready to go when the Svensons came. There had been a great deal to do. She did not seem to need sleep that night; it was as though she slept while she worked. All the time she knew that David was hurt, suffering, and that he was not coming back to her soon; she knew that she was left alone to take care of the baby and herself in a world capable of any monstrous and unpredictable cruelty. But the shock had made her numb, so that she did not feel much.

She washed clothes and bedding, and hung them out to dry by starlight. She sorted the remaining supplies and packed them neatly, to leave. She cleaned the stove and rubbed it and the stovepipe with kerosene to keep them from rusting. The last drop of oil from the lantern was poured into the kerosene can and the can's spout sealed with a potato. Her clothes and the baby's she made into two bundles, and in a box she packed the Bible, Tennyson's Poems, her sewing things and knitting needles, the brown silk, and the shell box David had given her. The pistol and its box of cartridges fitted neatly into a corner. She emptied the hay out of the bedtick, shook and brushed it and folded it neatly on the bare bunk. Quilts and blankets she stacked to take with her. There was a taste of brass in her mouth and her eyelids felt sandy, but she was not tired.

The baby was limp in sleep when she dressed him. Everything was ready when the Svensons came; she had only to put on her bonnet and padlock the door.

Mr. Svenson carried the box and bundles up the path; she snapped the padlock shut and followed with the baby.

The prairie was dark. The covered wagon and the oxen loomed against paler darkness. A chill breeze was stirring. Molly felt neither asleep nor awake while the jogging wagon took her away from the snug dugout, the creek, the plum trees, the haystacks by the sod barn, the well in the slough.

Dawn came across empty country, and sleepily Molly and Mrs. Svenson got down from the wagon and walked. They went so far ahead that they stopped to wait for the slow oxen. Molly sat on the ground and nursed the baby. The sun was higher now; the land had lost its contours. Flat and shadowless, it extended forever into distances, yet it was a mere platform in the infinite airiness of space.

When the plodding oxen brought up the wagon,

Molly laid the baby in it. He slept on the pile of bedding, rocking a little to the motion of the wheels. The imprisoned bees hummed in the hives. A mist of dust rose around the wagon, but Molly stayed close to it, so that she would hear the baby when he waked.

Part of the time Mrs. Svenson carried him. Once Mr. Svenson suggested that they ride a little way, but Molly shook her head. The load was heavy and for a long time the oxen had eaten nothing but hay. They often stopped to let the oxen rest. At noon they made a little fire of buffalo chips and Molly boiled tea. In the shadow of the wagon they drank it and ate cold boiled potatoes with salt, bread and molasses, and good raw turnips.

Almost all the afternoon they could see the town ahead. The railroad embankment and the buildings detached themselves from the horizon and came nearer with every mile. Now and then a scurry of dust followed a rider east or west. A team and buggy moved antlike on the prairie. Two men came riding out of the northwest, the outlaw country. For a moment they rode beside the wagon. Their eyes swept keenly over it and the oxen; they spoke to Mr. Svenson and went, with a clatter and diminishing rhythm of hoofs.

In the dusk a glimmer ahead took form as a lighted window. Buildings rose tall and square against the sky. Voices were heard; a door slammed. Molly nerved herself to approach this populous place. The wagon passed the side of a building and the street came suddenly out of the dusk.

It was intimidating. Half a dozen glass windows shed light on high porches where knots of men stood talking. A burst of shouts and laughter came from the saloon. Its door opened, spilling out noise, and two men swung onto horses and rode clattering away.

Two little boys came out of the dark and stood watching while Mr. Svenson unyoked and fed the oxen, and Mrs. Svenson made the camp fire. Molly sliced the rest of the boiled potatoes into a skillet. The hungry, tired baby began to whimper, and she hurried.

"Is he your husband?" one of the little boys asked her. .

"No." Molly nodded toward Mrs. Svenson. "He's hers."

"Is that their baby?"

"No, .he's my baby!" She straightened up and smiled.

"Then where's your husband?"

The innocent question pierced through her numbness. She felt a pain worse than physical agony, an anguish screaming for David. Screaming, shrieking, unbearable anguish of being less than whole, torn asunder, bereft.

"Well, I guess you got a husband, haven't you?" the little boy said.

Molly gasped. She turned upon the little boy, trying to speak. He stumbled backward, and words tore themselves harshly through her throat: "Yes, I have a husband! He's in the East."

The little boys were silent, and silently, after a moment, they went away.

Molly crawled into the wagon. She gathered the baby into her arms and rested against the piled bedding. The darling baby nuzzled and gurgled at her breast, and a tear ran down her cheek. She brushed it quickly away; tears are bad for babies.

When he was asleep, she tried, for his sake, to eat. But she could choke down only a few mouthfuls, she was drugged with weariness, and as soon as she had helped to wash the dishes and make the bed in the wagon, she took off her shoes and dress and lay down. She was numb again, but her mind was busy: Twenty dollars . . . Of course she must find work . . . the baby . . .the long winter . . . this strange town. . . Twenty dollars and the baby and six months of cold . . . but she was strong and willing. Her busy mind held her between sleep and waking. She was aware of the baby and Mrs. Svenson with her in the feather bed. The thin arch of canvas did not shut out the strangeness of noises made by human beings in the night. Even when the last horse galloped away, when the last door slammed, the town was still there, a disturbing sense that other people were near.

She heard Mr. Svenson roll from his blanket on the ground. He stamped into his boots and led the oxen away to water them. Dawn was gray under the wagon top. Molly put on her shoes and struggled into her dress.

In daylight the town was less intimidating than it

had been by night. The tall fronts of the buildings were thin boards; they had behind them only shanties, boarded up and down. The buildings tried to assert their importance, erecting painful vertical lines where all lines were low and level. But the great sky and the prairie ignored them. Barns, haystacks and a few little shanties straggled out and dwindled against the prairie, like a confession of futility.

Surely, Molly thought, among so many people, under so many roofs, she could find shelter for the baby and herself.

After breakfast she took the baby in her arms and set out. Mrs. Svenson, sympathetic and anxious, went with her. The Svensons had come out of their way to bring Molly to the town site; they had given her a day and were giving her another, out of the meager sum of days in which to make the long trip to Minnesota. Two days the oxen were eating their feed without coming nearer the journey's end. Molly was burdened by this kindness; it was too much to take, but she could not refuse it. She would not take more; today she would find winter shelter in the town.

There was the lumberyard—a stack of boards and a hill of coal glinting black in the sunlight. There was a barber shop; they passed it quickly, averting their eyes. There was a store with its front boarded up. Then the studding of a building, abandoned unfinished. The saloon was next.

They hurried, turning their heads and looking at the dusty street and the gaunt depot. Steel rails were laid, but trains would not be running till spring. A stale, cool smell of beer and whisky came from the saloon, and a man in shirt sleeves lounged at the door.

There was the store. Molly drew a deep breath and shifted the baby on her shoulder. He was wide awake, squirming, and his soft fist fumbled at her neck. Once, in the springtime that seemed so long past, David had brought her to the town site; she had seen Mr. and Mrs. Henderson and spoken to them. But it took all her resolution to go into the store. She had always been shy.

Mr. Henderson stopped urging a litter of dust and cigar stubs along the splintery floor, and leaned the broom against a nail keg. He was lean and a little stooped, so that his suspenders pulled straight from trousers to shoulders. "Good morning, ladies. What can I do for you this fine large morning?"

He did not recognize Molly at first and she was ashamed that she had not come to buy anything. Somehow she could not say that David was hurt. She told Mr. Henderson she wanted to stay in town till he came back. "I thought you might know where baby and I could stay. If I could work, perhaps, to help pay our way—— David sent me some money, but——"

Mr. Henderson tugged his beard. "Tell the truth, there's not many women folks left in town. Men with families mostly cleared out after the grasshoppers hit us. Mrs. Henderson, now—we're kind of crowded, but you might ask her. Anything suits her, suits me." He opened the door into the back room and called,

"Ma! Here's a couple ladies to see you! . . . Go right in."

Mrs. Henderson was getting breakfast. Two pig-tailed little girls were setting the table, and in the lean-to shed a little boy splashed at the washbasin. A bed, a trundle bed and a pallet were visible through another door. Mrs. Henderson was small, quick and voluble. She asked Molly and Mrs. Svenson to sit down and excuse her if she went on with her work. The teakettle hummed, stove lid and skillet clattered, frying salt pork sputtered and smoked.

"Well, of course you can't stay by yourself on a claim, and winter coming on! There's not many men'll do it. Let's see. I'd be glad to take you in my-self—goodness knows a little board money'd help out —but you see how it is: just the one bedroom for the six of us, and when it's our turn to board the school-teacher I'll have to make down a bed for her here in the kitchen. One mercy: the cookstove'll keep us warm. Not but what we'll burn hay, the price coal is! We expected to have us a house built before this, but what with grasshoppers and these hard times—— That's the baby yelling . . . Evangeline, you go tend to him." One of the little girls went into the dim bedroom. "Well, let's see. Now there's Mrs. Decker the saloon keeper's wife, but a good pious woman. She has only the one room, but it's good-sized, and nobody but her and her husband. She could put up a curtain; she'll have to for the teacher anyway. Then there's Mr. Insull—he's going to be the station agent; they're out here taking care of company tools.

She could take you in as well as not. I don't know if she'd take a boarder—she's high-toned and they've got his salary—but no harm trying."

Breakfast was on the table and Mrs. Henderson urged them to take potluck.

Mr. Henderson came in and said hospitably, "Sit right up and don't be bashful! Plenty more down cellar in a teacup!"

Molly said no, thank you, they had already had breakfast.

Mrs. Henderson went into the street with them, to point out Mrs. Decker's shanty. "If you don't find what you're looking for, you come right back here. My land, you've got to have some place. I guess we'll manage to squeeze you in somehow."

There was a cigar store, closed. There was the Livery, Sale and Feed stable. One buggy stood in it, the shafts uplifted with an air of helplessness, and only two horses were in the row of empty stalls.

Molly and Mrs. Svenson walked down the dusty road to Mrs. Decker's shanty. It had a glass window, with curtains. A few bits of dead bean vine still clung to the strings that went up the walls. Mrs. Decker was a thin, sallow woman with bright black eyes and sun-dried hair pulled tightly back from her forehead. She stood in the doorway and looked sharply at Molly, the baby, Molly's wedding ring.

"Your husband's in the East, you say? Whereabouts in the East?"

"Iowa."

"Why's he staying in Iowa? Why isn't he here taking care of you? I don't know what he'd leave you out here for, in the first place!"

"He went East to work," Molly repeated. "He's coming back as soon as he can." It seemed to her that it was not she, not herself, standing before a door and answering questions asked by a strange woman. Her arms were tired and the baby jiggled up and down.

"Well, I'd have to ask my husband. Mrs. Henderson sent you, you say?"

"Yes."

"I guess it's all right, but I'd have to ask him. What would you be willing to pay?"

"I want to pay what it's worth. But I——"

"Well, come in," said Mrs. Decker.

The shanty was large and nicely furnished. There was a bedstead, a table and benches, the cookstove and a rocking-chair. It was not a hickory chair but a boughten one. The mark of a rope across its wooden back was partly hidden by a crocheted tidy. Crocheted lace edged the window curtains made of flour sacks. The bed was covered with a spotless sheet; there were pillow shams at its head, and splashers hung on the rough board walls behind the stove and above the washbasin bench. They were made of flour sacks embroidered in red thread. The splashers had flowers and birds on them; the pillow shams said "Good Night" and "Sweet Dreams."

"I hope the baby wouldn't make much trouble," Mrs. Decker said.

"No. He hardly ever cries," Molly said. Mrs. Svenson began eagerly to praise the good baby.

Mrs. Decker interrupted: "Well, I only hope he don't cry in the mornings. Mr. Decker has to get his rest. . . We could put your bed behind a curtain in that corner. Have you a bedstead?"

"No. I have bedding."

"Well, I wasn't brought up to have beds on the floor. But I guess it can't be helped. You'd be willing to sleep with the school-teacher when it's our turn to keep her?"

Molly did not want to sleep with a stranger. "Yes," she said.

"Well. Could you pay four dollars a week?"

Molly was stunned. She looked wide-eyed at Mrs. Decker.

"You're eating for two, and everything's high. It has to be hauled in. Nobody made a crop this year, and the grasshoppers took our garden. I don't see how I could do it for less. There's coal to buy too. You can't expect to be warm all winter for nothing."

There was not enough work in the place for two women. And Mrs. Decker was a woman who would do all her own work, because nobody else could do it to suit her.

"Of course, if you can't pay——" Mrs. Decker said. "I wouldn't turn even a dog from my door that hadn't any other place to go."

Molly said with dignity, "It's a little more than I wanted to pay, but I will think about it. Good morning, Mrs. Decker."

In the doorway Mrs. Decker seemed about to say something more, but shut her lips together and didn't. Mrs. Svenson took the baby.

There was only the dwindling road and the prairie beyond Mrs. Decker's shanty. Between it and the livery stable there were two deserted shanties and two which revealed plainly enough that men were baching in them.

It seemed unreal to Molly that she was walking on the dusty road, in this strange town, homeless. Two black horses came dashing past the lumberyard, drawing behind them a buggy and a swirl of dust. In front of the store a young man wrapped the lines around the whip and jumped out of the buggy. Face to face with Molly, he halted, swept off his hat, snatched the cigar from his mouth and threw it away.

"Good morning, ma'am! Get your letter all right?" He was the young rider she had stopped on the prairie and asked to bring her the letter from David.

"Good morning," she said. "Yes, thank you."

"Second time I asked for it, they told me Two Gun Pete got it."

"Thank you just the same."

"Don't mention it, ma'am."

It was all a dream. People come and go like that in dreams, without reason or purpose. In a dream one has this heavy burden on the heart, a sense of loss and woe deeper and wider than thought. In a dream Mrs. Svenson plods beside you, dumb with sympathy and concern, and Mr. Svenson sits by his covered wagon patiently waiting. Molly knew she must do something.

Mrs. Insull lived upstairs above the depot. It was the only two-story building in town. The rough stairs went up from the waiting room, where Mr. Insull and another man were storing the company's tools for the winter.

"Go right up and knock," he said.

Molly summoned all her resolution. Bravely, with a faintness in her middle, she went up the stairs. The door stood before her, knowing what lay beyond it and stolidly refusing to tell. She would not let it terrify her; she rapped upon it. Mrs. Insull opened the door. Mrs. Insull was cleaning house. She had been working with fury and she was in a temper. A towel was around her head, a mop in her hand, and a swirl of soapy water lay behind her between the wet boards of the floor and the dry.

The room revealed such luxury as Molly had never seen. The wall was covered with a flowery paper, and all the furniture pushed back against it was shiny boughten furniture. Chairs, sofa, a center table, a tall lamp, velvet and painted roses were a confused magnificence behind Mrs. Insull.

"Good morning. I'm looking for work," Molly said.

"Well, there's plenty of it here! But if you think I can afford a hired girl, you're mistaken!" Mrs. Insull replied tartly. "If we could even afford to live decently we'd never've come to this country in the first place."

"I'd work for my keep," Molly said.

"You're with the campers down the street, aren't you?"

"No. Yes. That is, this is my friend Mrs. Svenson; I came to the town site with them, but——"

"Well, take my advice and keep right on going east with them. This country's gone to the dogs, if you ask me. The sooner you get out of it the better for you. I can't ask you in, I'm busy; but it wouldn't be any use. We've got three growing boys to feed and not enough left over to keep a cat. Not that there's a cat in the whole country, and mice eating us out of house and home. So, if you'll excuse me——" She was shutting the door.

"Good morning," said Molly. She turned and took the baby from Mrs. Svenson. Holding him to her fiercely, she marched down the stairs, across the waiting room, out of that place. Mrs. Svenson hurried beside her, bewildered and troubled; she had not understood the rapid words. She wrung her hands, asking what Molly was to do.

"I'm going home," Molly said. She felt she should never have budged from the homestead. David's wife, David's baby being offered charity, having doors closed in their faces! While David, far away, was hurt and helpless. David had made a home for her and she would stay in it. If she had to face loneliness, cold, wolves, outlaws, she'd face them. She'd stay there; she'd be right there when David came back.

Mrs. Svenson's worried opposition became frantic without touching her. She was going home. She couldn't let the Svensons lose another day, taking her home. But she was going. She felt, thought, heard nothing but that single furious impluse. The young man was coming out of the store. Awkwardly he tried to balance packages and reach his hat.

"Is that your team and rig?" Molly asked him.

"You bet!" he answered proudly.

"You know where I live. Would you take me out there for a dollar?"

"You bet I would!"

Mr. Svenson tried to use his masculine authority, saying he was responsible to David for her safety. Mrs. Svenson pleaded and begged, almost crying. If there was no place for her at the town site, they would take her with them to the refuge in Minnesota. Molly didn't even consider such a voyage into the unknown, where David must search to find her; their homestead would be lost before they could get back to it. The one idea of reaching home possessed her. Nothing could have stopped her.

Prudently, carefully, she bought supplies for the winter. Mr. Henderson expostulated weakly, but knew it wasn't up to him to interfere with what was none of his affair. She thanked the Svensons with all her heart. She would never see them again, her only friends, and she kissed Mrs. Svenson as she had kissed her sisters when she left them forever to come west with David.

Then she was speeding over the prairie behind the swift black team. Their flashing hoofs, their manes and tails blowing in the wind, the air rushing against

90

her face, and this strange young man beside her, were the last fantasy of that incredible day. She rested in a kind of stupor, waiting for this dream to end.

After a few remarks, the young man, too, was silent. His name was Dan Gray. He had said with no affected modesty that he owned the best team west of Council Bluffs, and would like to see the man who could beat him handling horses. The sky line did not change, but within it the prairie whirled past in inconceivable rapidity. In the distance Molly could see the dots that were the haystacks and the sod barn. Absently the young man began to sing; he stopped at once, shocked by his impoliteness. Like David, he wanted to sing when he was driving across the wide prairie. Molly said, "Do sing. I like it."

The sun was sinking in a chill apricot glow, the baby slept on her tired arm, and she was carried onward smoothly and swiftly as in a dream, while the young man buoyantly sang the jolly song:

Oh, when I left my eastern home, so
    happy and so gay,
To try to win my way to wealth
    and fame,
I little thought that I'd come down to
    burning twisted hay,
In a little old sod shanty on a
    claim!

Oh, the hinges are of leather, the
    windows have no glass,
And the roof it lets the howling
    blizzards in.

And I hear the hungry coyote as he
sneaks up through the grass,
'Round my little old sod shanty
on the claim!

My clothes are plastered o'er with
dough, I'm looking like a fright,
And everything is scattered 'round
the room,
And I fear if P.T. Barnum's man
should get his eye on me,
He would take me from my little
cabin home.

Oh, the hinges are of leather, the
windows have no glass,
And the roof it lets the howling
blizzards in——

"I like that song," Molly said. "Have you a sod shanty?"

"You bet! Two rooms and a lean-to. My claim's four miles west of the town site. Grasshoppers cleaned me out this year, but I can winter the team through and buy seed."

"You're doing well."

"Yes, I'm in pretty good shape." He paused. "I got a girl too."

"That's nice." Molly smiled. She liked **Mr. Gray** and was glad he was doing so well.

"She's about your age. I'd like to bring her out to see you folks some Sunday. We go driving on Sundays. This team'll cover forty miles and come in as fresh as daisies."

Molly thought that some day David would have his driving team and buggy. The Svensons were gone, but here were other friends already. Neighbors were not so far away, when a driving team could go forty miles on Sunday.

There was the well in the slough, the haystacks, the barn, all strangely unchanged. Mr. Gray carried her bundles and box, and held the baby while she turned the key in the padlock. The dugout was bleak with packed stores and bare bunk, but it was home.

"You got a snug place here," Mr. Gray said.

"We like it." Molly could hardly keep awake. Mr. Gray brought in the supplies she had bought. He fetched a pail of water from the well. He asked if he could do anything else, and when Molly thanked him and gave him the dollar, he took it as if he didn't like to.

"Kind of hate to leave you out here alone, but I guess it's safe enough for a while, with this good weather. When's your husband coming back?"

"I don't know exactly."

"You got a gun and know how to use it?"

"Yes."

"Likely you won't have any trouble, but it's just as well—— Ada and I'll be driving out this way next Sunday if the weather's fine. Well, so long!"

He was gone. Molly got the pistol from the box and loaded it with fingers that had no feeling in them. She spread the bedding on the bunk, undressed in a daze, and lay down with the baby. "Well, little David John, here we are," she thought, and she fell sound asleep.

The baby awakened her a few times; except for these interruptions she slept sixteen hours, and next day the familiar objects about her gave her a sense of security. She felt that she would get through the winter all right. Now and then a man stuck it out on a lonely homestead; why shouldn't she? "Dear Wife, do the best you can," David had written; yet, in a panic she had almost abandoned the homestead. David might have come back penniless in the spring to find her a hired girl and claim jumpers in possession of their home. It was much wiser to stay on it. The baby would be company for her, and wherever she was she must somehow bear the half life of living without David.

That week she wrote him a long letter, which she meant to ask Mr. Gray to take to the post office in town. She would not worry David telling him that the Svensons had gone. With a pen she was more articulate than with words; she wrote him that she loved him. She wrote about the baby's tooth and Mr. Svenson's cutting the hay on shares. The money he had sent was ample; she and the baby were in the best of health and wanted for nothing. Mr. and Mrs. Svenson were kndness itself, and all was snug for the winter. And carefully, in her delicate writing, every letter precisely slanted, she wrote,

We are having hard times now, but we should not dwell upon them but think of the future. It has never been easy to build up a country, but how much easier it is for us, with such great comforts and conveniences, kerosene, cookstoves, and even railroads and fast posts, than it was for our forefathers. I trust that, like our own parents, we may live to see times more prosperous than they have ever been in the past, and we will then reflect with satisfaction that these hard times were not in vain.

This letter, carefully folded, sealed and addressed, was never mailed. It lay all winter between the pages of the Bible, for the weather changed suddenly. Saturday morning was mild as May; Saturday afternoon a dark cloud rose from the northwest. It hung across the sky for a time, with an ominous feathery undercloud. Then, like a solid white wall, the blizzard advanced. With the snow came the winds, howling.

Let the hurricane roar!
   It will the sooner be o'er!
We'll weather the blast
      and land at last,
On Canaan's happy shore!

IV

THREE days and nights the winds did not cease to howl, and when Molly opened the door she could not see the door ledge through swirling snow. How cold it was she could not guess. At sight of the cloud she had hurriedly begun cramming every spare inch of the dugout with hay. Twisted hard, it burned with a brief, hot flame. Her palms were soon raw and bleeding from handling the sharp, harsh stuff, but she kept on twisting it; she kept the dugout warm.

In the long dark hours—for she was frugal with kerosene; a wavering light came from the drafts and the broken lid of the stove—she began to fight a vague and monstrous dread. It lay beneath her thoughts; she could not grasp it as a whole; she was always aware of it and never able to defeat it. It lay shapeless and black in the depths of her. From time to time it flung up a question:

What if the baby gets sick?

"He won't be sick!" she retorted. "He's a strong, healthy baby. If he's sick, I'll take care of him. "I'd take care of him anyway; there's no doctor in town."

Suppose something has happened to David? Suppose he never comes back?

"Be still! I won't listen."

That was like a wolf's howl in the wind. Wolves?

"Nonsense, I have the gun. How could a wolf get through the door?"

When you go out—— If a wolf sprang suddenly—— what of the baby, alone in the dugout?

"Why am I scaring myself with horrible fancies? Nothing like that will happen."

She could never conquer the shapeless, nameless dread itself. Silenced, it did not leave her. It would begin again.

What if the baby gets sick?

"Oh, stop, stop! I can't stand this!" her spirit cried out in anguish. And she asked herself angrily, "What is the matter with you? Brace up and show a little decent spunk! It's only a storm; there'll be lots of them before spring." She tried to conquer the shapeless, dark thing by ignoring it.

The wind howled, gray darkness pressed against the paper pane, a little hard snow, dry as sand, was forced through the crack beneath the door.

On the fourth morning Molly was awakened by an immense, profound silence. The frosty air stung her nostrils; the blanket was edged with rime from her breath. Snug in the hollow of her body the baby slept cozily. The window was a vague gray in the dark. She lighted the lamp and started a fire in the cold stove.

She was not perturbed until she tried to open the

door. Something outside held it against her confident push. And suddenly wild terror possessed her. She felt a Thing outside, pressed against the door.

It was only snow. She said to herself that it was only snow. There was no danger; the ledge was narrow. She flung all her strength and weight against the door. The stout planks quivered; they pressed against a crunching and a squeaking, and from top to bottom of them ran a sound like a derisive scratch of claws. Then snow fell down the abrupt slope below the ledge, and sunlight pierced Molly's eyes.

Taking the shovel, she forced her body through the narrow aperture she had gained. For an instant the pain in her eyes blinded her. Then she saw the immensity of whiteness and dazzling blue. She confronted space.

Under the immeasurably vast sky, a limitless expanse of snow refracted the cold glitter of the sun. Nothing stirred, nothing breathed; there was no other movement than the ceaseless interplay of innumerable and unthinkably tiny rays of light. Air and sun and snow were the whole visible world—a world neither alive nor dead, and terrible because it was alien to life and death, and ignorant of them.

In that instant she knew the infinite smallness, weakness, of life in the lifeless universe. She felt the vast, insensate forces against which life itself is a rebellion. Infinitely small and weak was the spark of warmth in a living heart. Yet valiantly the tiny heart continued to beat. Tired, weak, burdened by its own fears and sorrows, still it persisted, indomitably it continued to exist, and in bare existence itself, without assurance of victory, even without hope, in its indomitable existence among vast, incalculable, lifeless forces, it was invincible.

Molly was never able to say, even in her own thoughts, what she knew when she first came out of the dugout after the October blizzard. It was a moment of inexpressible terror, courage and pride. She was aware of human dignity. She felt that she was alive, and that God was with life. She thought: "The gates of hell shall not prevail against me." She could feel what David felt, singing: "Let the hurricane roar! We'll weather the blast."

She drew a deep breath, and with her shovel she attacked the snow. The winds had packed it hard as ice against the door and the creek bank. The path was buried under a slanting drift. Inch by inch, pounding, digging, scraping, lifting, she made a way on which she could safely walk, and that scratch on the illimitable waste of trackless snow was a triumph.

A blizzard of such severity so early in October seemed to predict an unusually hard winter. She could not know when the next storm might strike, and her first care was fuel. She dug into the snow-covered stacks by the barn, and tying a rope around big bundles of hay, she dragged them one by one down the path and into the dugout.

When she threw out the water in which she washed her hands, she noticed that its drops tinkled on the ice crust. They had frozen in the air. Startled, she looked into the mirror. Her nose and ears were white, and she had to rub them with snow till they painfully thawed.

Then for three weeks the weather was mild, the snow was melting. There were days when the door stood open and the air was like spring. From above the dugout she could see the town; she could, indeed, see fifty miles beyond it. But her letter remained unmailed. The nice Mr. Gray and his Ada did not come; perhaps he had no sleigh, perhaps they dared not venture so far from shelter, lest another blizzard catch them.

In early November the winter settled down. Blizzard followed blizzard out of the northwest. Sometimes there was a clear day between them, sometimes only a few hours. As soon as the winds ceased their howling and the snow thinned so that she could see, she went out with the shovel.

The wind would be steadily blowing, driving a low scud of snow before it. She worked sometimes waist deep in blown snow so thick that she could not see her feet. The whole world seemed covered with white spray flying under the cold sunshine. Her eyes were bloodshot and her skin burned red and blistered, and she never came into the dugout without looking to see if face and ears were frozen.

On the dark days of the blizzards she twisted hay; she lighted the lamp for cleaning and cooking and washing. And she played with the baby.

He was older now; he watched the gleams of firelight and clapped his hands, and his soft little palms hardly ever missed each other. His blue eyes looked into Molly's, his firm little body had a will of its own. He could hold up his own head proudly; he could straighten his backbone; all by himself he could sit up, and he could crawl. Kicking and crowing, he burbled sounds almost like words. "Mama," she could hear him say.

"Papa," she urged him. "Say it, baby dumpling! Say 'papa.' "

"Blablub!" he replied triumphantly, giving her a roguish glance that melted her heart. Kneeling by the bunk, she squeezed his wriggling body between her raw hands, she rolled and tumbled him and buried her rough face in his softness, in the warm perfume of his baby body. His fist tugged painfully at her hair and she laughed, teasing his nose with the loosened ends. She had begun to be almost as gay as David. She wondered, "Is David gay because he's frightened, because he has to be brave?"

There was always the ache of incompleteness without him. The shapeless dread might at any moment stab her with a question. But day by day the baby and she survived, and in the dugout the howling winds, the cold and snow and dark could not touch them. Her gayety was a defiance.

Then came the seven days' blizzard. There had been only a few hours of clear weather, but Molly had worked desperately; she had enough hay for three days and she had never known a blizzard to last longer. On the third day she burned the hay sparingly, but she was not alarmed. On the fourth day she broke up and burned a box, keeping the stove barely warm. On the fifth day she burned the remaining box. The heavy benches and table were left, and the cradle; in her folly she had left the ax in the barn.

She sat wrapped in blankets on the edge of the bunk. When the fire went out there was no light at all. The window was obscurely gray, a dim and unnaturally square eye, looking in upon her. The stout door shook to the pounding and prying of yelling winds. And time was lost, so that she did not know whether this were day or night, nor how long those winds had possessed all space. She had so long hoped to hear their energy exhausted that it seemed to her inexhaustible. The tiny pocket of still air in the dugout was increasingly cold.

If she and the baby lay close together under blankets, they could exist for some time in the warmth of their own bodies. If this were to go on forever—— It could not, of course. Feebly she gave up the problem of the heavy benches, which she could not break up with her hands. It must be the cradle. But she feared to burn it so soon.

During the seventh day she smashed and frugally burned the cradle. The birds that David had carved helped to boil tea and potatoes. She mashed a potato in a little hot water and fed it with a spoon to the baby. Then she put out the lamp and lay down with him under all the bedding.

A change in the sound of the wind awakened her. She did not know whether it was night or day, but when she forced the door open she saw a whiteness of driven snow. A fierce north wind was driving the flakes steadily before it, and Molly's relief was like a shout of joy. The snow was not swirling; the blizzard was over!

When next she opened the door, the storm had diminished so that she could see vaguely into it. She was able to clear the path, and when she reached its top she could see dim shapes of barn and haystacks. The wind almost took her off her feet, and when she had a bundle of hay and was dragging it through the soft drifts, she had to fight it as though it were a live thing struggling to get away.

After she had filled the dugout with hay, she stretched a rope from the barn to the top of the path, so that she could fetch fuel, if necessary, during a blizzard.

Vaguely through the storm she seemed to see a dark patch on the opposite bank of the creek. It troubled her, for she could not imagine what it might be; perhaps an illusion of eyes weeping in the wind, perhaps some danger against which she should defend herself. She shut the door against it hurriedly and gave herself to the marvel of warmth and rest.

In the morning, in dazzling glitter of sun on snow, she saw across the creek a herd of cattle. Huddled together, heads toward the south and noses drooping to their knees, they stood patiently enduring the cold. In terror she thought of the haystacks. The creek bank hid them from the cattle now, but if the herd moved southeast, across the slough, and saw that food, would all the strength of the wind prevent them from turning and destroying her fuel?

She put on her wraps and took the pistol. Not with pitchfork or ax, she knew, could she keep starving cattle from food. Nor did she dare risk facing the stampede. She could only try to turn it with shots, and, failing, take refuge in the barn. If the fuel were lost——

The cattle did not move. It came to her, while she watched, that for a long time they had not moved. Yesterday she had seen the herd, huddled motionless in the storm. This prodigy, this incredible fact of cattle not moving before a storm, chilled her thought. She stared at them—gaunt sides and ridged backbones, dropped necks and lax tails, motionless as if carved. Were they dead—frozen? No; breath came white from their nostrils.

The thought that they might be dead had brought a vision of meat.

Her courage quailed. There was something monstrous, something that gave her an unreasoning terror, like a breath of the supernatural, in this herd of motionless cattle. Her jaw clenched against the cold, she went slowly, knee-deep in drifts, down the bank and across the frozen creek. Was this too great a risk? Leaving the baby in the dugout and venturing into she knew not what? The cattle did not move. She went within ten yards of them, five, two. They did not even lift their heads.

Over their eyes—thick over their eyes and hollowed temples—were cakes of ice. When she saw this, she understood. Their own breath, steaming upward while they plodded before the storm, had frozen and blinded them.

In a rage of pity, an outbursting cry against the universal cruelty, she plunged through the snow to the nearest patiently dying creature; she wrenched the ice from its eyes. The steer snorted; he flung up his head in terror, and ran, staggering. The herd quivered. A few yards away, the steer stopped, hesitated in fear of the loneliness around him, and turned back uncertainly toward the herd. A long bawl of misery came from his throat. Then he, too, let his head droop.

Molly knew what she must do. She thought of the baby, drawing his strength from hers. She held all thought, all feeling, firmly to the baby, and walking to the nearest young steer, she put the pistol to his temple, shut her eyes and fired. The report crashed through her.

She felt the shudder of all the beasts. When she opened her eyes they had not moved. The steer lay dead, only a little blood trickling, freezing, from the wound. And perhaps it had been merciful to kill him.

Then, like an inspiration, a revival of all gay hope, she thought of a cow. The cow! Why not? In the herd there were many cows. Alas, they belonged to somebody. To whom? She did not know; that might never be known; impossible to guess how many miles —hundreds, perhaps—they had been driven by the storm. But they were branded. She could not steal. Yet, if she did not take one of these cows, would it not die? The whole blinded herd was helpless and dying. To kill for food was permissible, but to steal? Was she a cattle thief? But a cow—to have a cow! Milk for the baby. To surprise David when he came home, with a cow!

She thought that perhaps there was a yearling that was not branded.

In her excitement she was almost laughing. Clumsy in boots and coat and shawls, she pushed into the harmless herd. The heifers, she knew, would be in the center. The old bull grumbled in his throat, shaking his blind head, but he did not move; he did not even paw the snow. There was a young heifer, unbranded, almost plump, a clear red all over. Molly marked it for her own, for their own cow.

This incredible marvel of good fortune filled her with laughing joy. What a triumph, what a joke—to take a cow from the blizzard, to take it from the very midst of a dangerous herd! And to have a cow—after so many calamities, in spite of calamities, to have a cow—this was a vindication of all confidence and hope.

She struggled through the drifts, across the creek, up the bank, to the dugout. She fed the stove with hay, she nursed the baby, dressed him warmly, wrapped him in blankets like a cocoon. Then she went to the barn for a rope.

The short winter day gave her not too much time. The sun was overhead before she had succeeded in prodding and tugging the terrified, wild, blinded heifer out of the herd. It clung with desperation to the safety of the herd, and she had still to get it across the

creek, up the bank and into the barn. Its strength—
greater than hers—wore her out. In one frantic
plunge and leap it undid the work of half an hour. Its
blindness was her only help and she thanked God for
the continued bitter cold. But often she stopped to
rub face and ears with snow, and beating her numb
hands on her chest did not keep the feeling in them.

It was near sunset before she got the heifer into the
barn. She put hay into the manger and tore the ice
from the heifer's eyes. With the rope and ax she went
back to the herd. She cut the best parts of meat from
the half-frozen carcass, and tied the pieces together.
Then, trembling in her weariness, she went from animal to animal, tearing off the blinding ice. The cattle
snorted and plunged; each one ran staggering a little
way and waited, bawling. Slowly the herd drifted before the wind. The sun sank in coldness, the glow
faded from the snow, and in the dusk she released the
old bull. He lifted his head, bellowed weakly, and
plunged staggering after the herd.

In the dark they would not see her hay. The wind
was blowing toward the town site; let the townspeople
deal with the survivors who reached it. Molly had
given the cattle a chance for their lives, and she felt
she had earned her cow.

The blizzard that came that night lasted only a
day. Molly lay cozily in bed. The baby gurgled and
kicked in exuberance of spirits; a great beef stew sim-
mered on the stove, filling the air with its fragrance.
The snowy hay in the manger would suffice the heifer
for both food and water. The howling of the blizzard

did not disturb Molly; she felt the braggart joy of Samson, hugging in secret his triumph. "A lion stood in the way; but out of the eater I have taken meat; out of the strong I have taken sweetness."

If only David could know that they had a cow! But now she was confident that David would come home strong and well; this winter would end, they would be together in the spring. And how good to lie on a soft hay tick, under warm blankets; how good to feel the heartening strength of meat stealing drowsily all through one's body; how good to be warm and to rest. She felt she had never been thankful enough for all her blessings.

Two haunches of the beef she had left outside the door, to freeze on the snow. The blizzard had buried them, and she did not touch the drift when she dug the path again. Snow was still falling thickly enough to fill the air as with a mist, through which she saw the barn and haystacks.

The heifer was still safely tied to the manger. It snorted and plunged, wild-eyed, while she brought in hay and set two pails of snow within its reach. She spoke to it soothingly, but did not touch it. In time it would learn her kindness and be gentle. It had all the marks of a good milch cow.

She closed the barn door and snapped the padlock, feeling a proud sense of property to be taken care of. There was no wind, and all around her she could hear the soft rustle of the falling snow. With the shovel and rope, she went toward the haystack. Afterward she always said she did not know what made her stop and turn around. By the corner of the barn stood a wolf.

If you went out—— If a wolf sprang—— What would become of the baby, alone in the dugout? *It's come,* her frozen heart knew.

She had only the shovel.

The wolf's haunches quivered, not quite crouching. The hair stood rough along its back. Fangs showed beneath the curling lip. It was a gaunt, big timber wolf. Its mate could not be far away. Its mate was perhaps creeping up behind her.

She dared not turn lest this one spring. Its eyes shone green in the half light. The snow sifted downward, a moving, transparent screen between her and those eyes. Snowflakes settled on the wolf's shaggy neck. His mouth opened in a soundless pant; the red tongue flicked hungrily over the pointed muzzle.

He shifted a paw. Molly did not move. Swiftly the wolf turned and vanished, a shadow, in the falling snow. The snow at once became a menace, hiding the lurking danger.

Molly walked steadily through the white blindness toward the dugout. She did not run; she knew that if she ran, her inmost self would yield to shattering terror. As long as the wolf could not be seen anywhere, she was safe; the wolf would not spring unless he could see her. But while she was going down the path in the creek bank, he might spring on her from above. She knew he was following her.

She reached the path and ran. There was no measure in time for the length of that distance from the edge of the prairie to the door's slamming behind her. A long wolf howl rose from the ceiling above her head. Another answered it from the frozen creek below.

Several times that day she faintly heard the heifer's desperate bawling. The barn door was solid; the walls were thick, and the roof, too, was of sod. Whether the wolves could scratch their way through it, she did not know. They were hungry; she had seen the fur hollowed between the ribs.

That evening she heard snarling and crunching at the door. The wolves had found the fresh meat. They must have been following the cattle, and the carcass of the steer she had killed had kept them near her. She heard a shuffling along the threshold, a scratch of claws on the door.

She kept the lamp lighted and sat all night watching the paper pane. The window space was too small to let a wolf through easily. If paw or head appeared, she was ready to shoot. The ax was in the dugout, and she decided, rather than go out in the snowstorm again, to chop up table and benches, and burn them. But she made the hay last two days, and then a sliver of brightness above the snow piled against the window told her that the sun was shining.

Little by little she forced the door open. The pistol was in her hand. She could not see the wolves. This did not mean that they might not we waiting beyond the edge of the bank above. But she could not survive all winter without fuel. Some dangers must be faced.

She found no trace of the wolves anywhere, and in the barn the heifer was safe. After that she often heard wolves howling, and found their tracks at the door and around the barn. She never left the dugout without the pistol. She made a belt in which to carry it, so that it was always ready to her hand while she was clearing the path or struggling with the bundles of hay.

The reality of the wolves constantly reminded her of David's warning. Wolves, he had written—and outlaws. When she stirred the fire she thought of the smoke ascending from the chimney. For seventy miles around, on clear days, it could be seen that the dugout was inhabited. Claim jumpers would probably not come. But outlaws?

She felt within herself a certainty that at any human threat of danger she would kill. She said to herself that no stranger should enter that dugout—not under any circumstances, not with any fair words. This she determined upon, sure of herself. But she did not yet know herself.

Blizzard followed blizzard, with clear hours or days between. She had lost reckoning of time and was not quite sure whether December had ended and January begun. But each day brought nearer the end of this winter. The baby was healthy, the heifer was safe in the barn, and she was holding out pretty well. More and more often she dreamed of springtime and David, beyond her reach, and she too confused or too weak to reach them, or to make David hear her calling to him. But in the daytime she knew she had only to hold on; David would come, spring would come; she did not need to go toward them.

February had come, though she did not know it. Three clear days of terrible cold were ending, near nightfall, in the rising of the blizzard winds. That day Molly had filled half the barn with hay; the heifer was now so gentle that she could turn it loose with that abundance of feed, and the washtub full of water provided for it if this blizzard lasted a week. The baby slept. The box was full of twisted hay, the supper dishes washed, and by the faint light of the dying fire Molly combed her hair for the night.

A blow struck the door, and all at once the forces of the air gave tongue. Molly thought how like demon riders they sounded, racing and circling overhead with unearthly, inhuman shriek and scream and wild halloo. A little snow, fine and hard as sand, was driven through the crack beneath the door. She shook her hair back and put her hands to braid it, and in the gleam of light from the broken stove lid she saw a joint of the stovepipe suddenly bend. The two ends of pipe slid upon each other, a crack opened between them. Petrified, she heard a human cry, a groaned exclamation.

A man was on top of the dugout. Blind in the storm, he had stumbled against the chimney. No honest man, no lost homesteader. Not for miles around was there an undeserted homestead. All afternoon the blizzard had been threatening; no honest man would have gone far from shelter. Only a rider out of the northwest might have fled before the storm. Out of the northwestern refuges of the outlaws. "Wolves and outlaws will be moving back to settled country."

He had struck the chimney on the eastern side; he was going toward the creek. Only a few steps and he would fall down the creek bank, down into the deep drifts below. He would be gone, lost, buried somewhere by the storm. Only his bones would be found after the snow melted in the spring. "Keep still!" she said. "Don't move. It isn't your business. Don't let him in. Who knows what he is, what he would do? Think of the baby. *What are you doing?*"

Her mouth close to the stovepipe, she shouted, "Stand still! Don't move!" The soot dislodged from the open joint of the pipe fell on her face, so quickly had she acted. "You hear me?" she called.

A vague shout replied. He seemed to have fallen or to have wandered a step or two toward the creek. She knew how the winds were swirling, beating and tugging at him from every side, how the sandlike snow was flaying his face; she saw him blinded, deafened, lost. An outlaw, but human, fighting the storm.

"Lie down! Crawl!" she shouted. "Creek bank ahead! Follow it to the right! The right! Find a rope! You hear?"

His shout was dull through the shriller winds. Then she hesitated. But the barn was padlocked. "There is a path!" she called. "Path! Down! To the left!"

If he shouted again, she did not hear him. She

twisted her hair and thrust pins into it, buttoned her basque and lighted the lamp. She got her pistol and made sure it was loaded. Some instinct, hardly reasonable—for who would harm a baby?—made her lift David John, wrap him in a blanket and lay him on the hay in the wood box. She felt better with the baby behind her. Then she lifted the bar on the door, and retreating behind the table, she waited.

She had time to regret what she had done, and to know that she could not have done otherwise.

The wind suddenly tore open the door. Snow whirled in, and cold. The lamp flared smokily, and as she started forward, the man appeared in the white blizzard. He was tall and shapeless in fur coat and cap and ear muffs caked with snow; he was muffled to reddened slits of eyes and snow-matted eyebrows; it was an instant before she knew him and screamed. The wild scream was dizzily circling in her head when his arms closed around her, hard and cold as ice.

"Oh, how—how—how did you get here?" she gasped after a while, unable still to believe it. Her hands kept clutching, clutching up and down the snowy fur, as if her hands were separate things, frantic too, to make sure this was David.

"Gosh, I'm freezing you to death! I got to shut the door," he said. And at these homely words, because David was shutting the door, she burst into tears.

"H-h-have you—had any supper?" she wept.

"Hang supper!" he sang out joyously.

Later he teased her a little. "What's so surprising? Didn't I tell you I'd get here quick as I could?" He scolded her seriously: "Molly, God only knows what I went through when they told me in town that Svensons had quit and you were out here alone. Don't you ever do another fool trick like that. Do you suppose I care a damn for anything in the world compared to you?"

He asked, "How's the little shaver?" and she said, "Oh, David, he's wonderful! He's got two teeth! Just ——" But then he hugged her, and there was so much to ask, to tell.

They had warned him in town that he couldn't beat the blizzard, but he thought he could make it. He had almost reached the slough when the storm struck. He must have been confused and gone the wrong way; he was looking for the well in the slough when he struck the chimney. "I thought from the well I could make the barn, and then the creek bank. But I thought I was going north. Then, when I hit the chimney, I didn't know where I was. I couldn't make out what it was. It just hit me, and then I couldn't find it again. That was what I was doing—looking for it—when I heard you. Molly, angel!"

"Oh," she told him, "and we've got a cow!"

"A—not our own cow?"

"Well, a heifer. A good, gentle, red heifer. She'll make a fine milker."

"But how did you ever—— Look," he said, "I've

got forty dollars. I want to tell you Roslyn's the whitest man in twenty counties. I didn't expect to have a penny left, but——"

"Oh, David, how's your leg?"

"Well, I have to favor it a little—you notice I've got you on the other knee. But it stood the walk pretty well; it'll be fine as ever for spring plowing."

"And you walked ten miles! Oh, David!"

"What did you think I'd do, and you out here?"

"David, the whole country's overrun with wolves."

"Fine. I'll get some good skins."

It didn't matter, really, what they said. They were together; everything was all right. She heard the clamor of the storm, all the demons shrieking; simply a blizzard, simply the winter weather on their farm.

A little sound made her turn; there was the baby! There was little David John, wide-awake, lifting himself up with his tiny fingers on the edge of the wood box. A spear of hay clung to his wave-curl of hair. He bounced once, and then, clearly, triumphantly, he spoke.

"Blablub!" he said. A dimple quivered in his cheek; then his mouth spread in David's wide grin, and there were the two white teeth.

"Look, David, look! Oh, did you hear him call you papa?"

Somehow, without quite thinking it, she felt that a light from the future was shining in the baby's face. The big white house was waiting for him, and the acres of wheat fields, the fast driving teams and swift buggies. If he remembered at all this life in the dug-out, he would think of it only as a brief prelude to more spacious times.

About the Author

ROSE WILDER LANE was born in 1886 on a claim in the Dakota Territory, the daughter of Almanzo James Wilder and Laura Ingalls Wilder, who later wrote the classic *Little House* books. Rose grew up in Mansfield, Missouri, and moved later to California, where, married, she began her career writing free-lance articles for a California newspaper. Her writing grew to include biography, travel, and fiction. Of all her novels, *Let the Hurricane Roar* is perhaps the best loved and most popular.